AF822583

Willow River Almanac

A Father Copes with Divorce and Nature

Willow River Almanac

A Father Copes with Divorce and Nature

John J. Koblas

Illustrated by John Stevens

North Star Press of St. Cloud, Inc.

Library of Congress Cataloging-in-Publication Data

Koblas, John J., 1942-

Willow River almanac : a father copes with divorce and nature / John Koblas ; illustrated by John Stevens.

p. cm.

ISBN 0-87839-151-7 (pbk.)

1. Divorce--Pschological aspects--Case studies. 2. Koblas, John J., 1942--- Divorce. 3. Koblas, John J., 1942---Diaries. 4. Divorced men--Diaries. 5. Willow River State Park (Wis.) I. Title.

HQ814 .K63 2000
306.89'092--dc21

00-058247

Copyright © 2000 John J. Koblas
All Rights Reserved.

Published by:
North Star Press of St. Cloud, Inc.
PO Box 451
St. Cloud MN 56302

Printed in the United States of America by:
Versa Press, Inc.
East Peoria, IL 61611

Illustrations by:
John Stevens
PO Box 9367
Daytona Beach, Florida 32120

ISBN: 0-87839-151-7

For Stacy, Stephanie, John and Sarah,
And in beloved memory of
Buttons (1983-1999)

Willow River Almanac

A Father Copes with Divorce and Nature

The End

I sincerely believe that true love never dies. It is reshaped, re-channeled and reexamined, but the emotion lingers long after it should be forgotten. Pain, a result of love gone astray, also knows no termination. It fades with time, but the aching endures even after the reason for that pain has been forgotten.

I guess I have always been shadowed by pain. I grew up with it in a warm but curious childhood. When I was eighteen years old, my only brother went out for a pizza and was killed by a drunk driver. Seven years later, my father, who was never able to cope with the loss of his oldest son, died from a heart attack. Hell, I even spent a miserable, soul-wrenching year in prison. Why? I don't know why, anymore than I know why our loved ones have to die, and we, the selfish, stay behind to feel sorry for ourselves.

It was not what I did but what I didn't do that resulted in my spending a year in Leavenworth. I have always held strong convictions against taking any training with a weapon, and I made my stand, even though it cost me many friends. I objected not upon religious grounds, but on moral convictions, and was told by the government that no such stand existed. I could have stayed out of prison. All that was needed was a signature from a minister stating I was a conscientious objector and member of a particular church. My father produced not one but two clergymen, both willing to sign the document in my favor. I was very ethical at the time and refused my freedom because it would have been the result of a lie. I was also a fool!

All I know is I went into that terrifying institution an immature young boy of twenty-four and came out a bitter, weary old man of twenty-five. During that tenure, I somehow learned to cope with despair and grew up a little quicker than I should have wanted. I guess, among other things, this was why my marriage was so important to me. Through love and sharing, my marriage was a means of keeping me focused on the future, and not in the past, and keeping my personal bitterness in check.

We were such a happy little family. Everything changed so quickly—very real nightmares I considered impossible—and we were soon swept up in a whirl of bitterness, deceit, and tears. My wife had been my life. She possessed a radiant smile, which she managed not only with her lips, for when she was herself, there was a captivating exuberance that glowed from her eyes. During those moments when her bright eyes smiled into mine, I saw myself in a world that was bathed in innocence and faith. There followed a pristine serenity and I felt safe, and loved, and lucky.

My oldest daughter, Stacy, was sixteen when my wife and I separated. She played piano and violin, wrote stories and poems. We would often sit at the kitchen table and write haiku, read what the other had written, and write more. When my wife did not care to attend the symphony or a museum, Stacy would always accompany me. I always remember one Christmas Eve, when as a baby, she attempted to follow me down the basement stairs, lost her footing and tumbled towards the cement floor below. I made a dive worthy of any shortstop and caught her coming over the last stair. It had been a close call but it made me realize how precious she was to me.

Stephanie, my second oldest at fourteen, was the life of the party. She joked, laughed, and made unbelievably silly faces and always brightened my horizons. Like her older sister, she too played piano as well as flute and clarinet. You couldn't keep her down. As a toddler she had broken her leg, and despite an unyielding cast, she ran around the house the very day we returned from the hospital. Stephanie too was so special to me—all my kids are—each in their very own way.

My son, John, who would be twelve that November, was another gem. If ever there was a dedicated young athlete, John was that hot prospect. He excelled in baseball, football, basketball, wrestling and was always the best in his age group. I really thought that one day his dedication would take him at least as far as professional minor league baseball. I coached his little league baseball and basketball teams and everything we did—win, lose, or draw—we did together.

Sarah, my youngest, would turn eight that November. I referred to her as "my little sweetheart," as she was eternally very affectionate and caring of others. As young as she was, she was already a responsible baby sitter, and like her sister Stephanie, quite a jokester. Each day when I came home, I looked forward to her smothering hugs and girlish giggles. She delighted in cooking meals for me, and I delighted in eating them. Whatever Sarah did, she did well.

It—the day Hell reared its ugly face—came during the summer of 1987. Never again would my life be the same nor anyone else's in my family. My wife, my partner, my best friend for so many years, filed for a legal separation that would lead to divorce. Initially, and for quite some time, I did not want to go on living. Had I been a weaker being (not that I was strong), I would not be writing these words today. The future then was a frightening entity more real than any horror novel I had read in all my forty-five years of existence. I could not face family, friends, and coworkers anymore than I could persuade myself to continue functioning. I needed to get my thoughts together and quickly.

This book then is not merely a book about divorce but an alternative for dealing with that divorce, as well as a statement about overcoming adversity. I quit my job, left Minneapolis in my van and, like Henry David Thoreau a century and a half before, went into the woods. I needed at least a month to myself, a month away from the sympathies and/or scorn of others, so I could rearrange my thoughts and make a feeble attempt at getting my life back together.

I found peace and serenity at Willow River State Park near Hudson, Wisconsin. For one month, despite the advent of winter, I lived in the woods recording flora, fauna, history, geology, feelings, and memories. This experiment in dealing with divorce through a brief but alternative lifestyle preserved my sanity. I still suffered the gnawing pain of a husband and father in turmoil, but, at least when I emerged from that woodland, I was able to live with that pain and face the world again. By enduring hardships, I learned that no matter how comfortable or successful we are in every day life, we must never take our situation for granted. While composing a diary for the thirty-one days of October I spent at Willow River in 1987, I learned to vent my feelings instead of allowing them to grow stale and bitter through idleness.

As I read my *Willow River Almanac* today, a decade later, the old hurts come back as if they occurred yesterday. My children have grown into adults and I have grown old in years, but I can still look back and remember all that I have never truly forgotten. I know the experiment of woodland isolation worked for me, and if the situation arose again today, I would go back to those woods. Yes, love and pain never die, but neither does the healing process. I would never have learned to cope with life if it were not for the trials and tribulations I endured at Willow River. One does not have to sit in an office and discuss a painful divorce with others. One merely has to be alone with his or her own pain. I wholeheartedly believe, as a result of my sojourn into isolation, that there is no better healing than that provided by Mother Nature.

This, then, is my *Willow River Almanac*—my day-to-day experiences coupled with my own emotions. The pain is evident but so, at times, is the shining star of hope. By standing up to hardships during an oncoming winter, I also learned to stand up to my situation and myself. Each person afflicted by the pain of separation must deal with divorce through his or her own method. Willow River gave me direction and a reason to go on. I can only share my thoughts with others through this diary. Only each individual can decide if there is a Willow River in his or her own life.

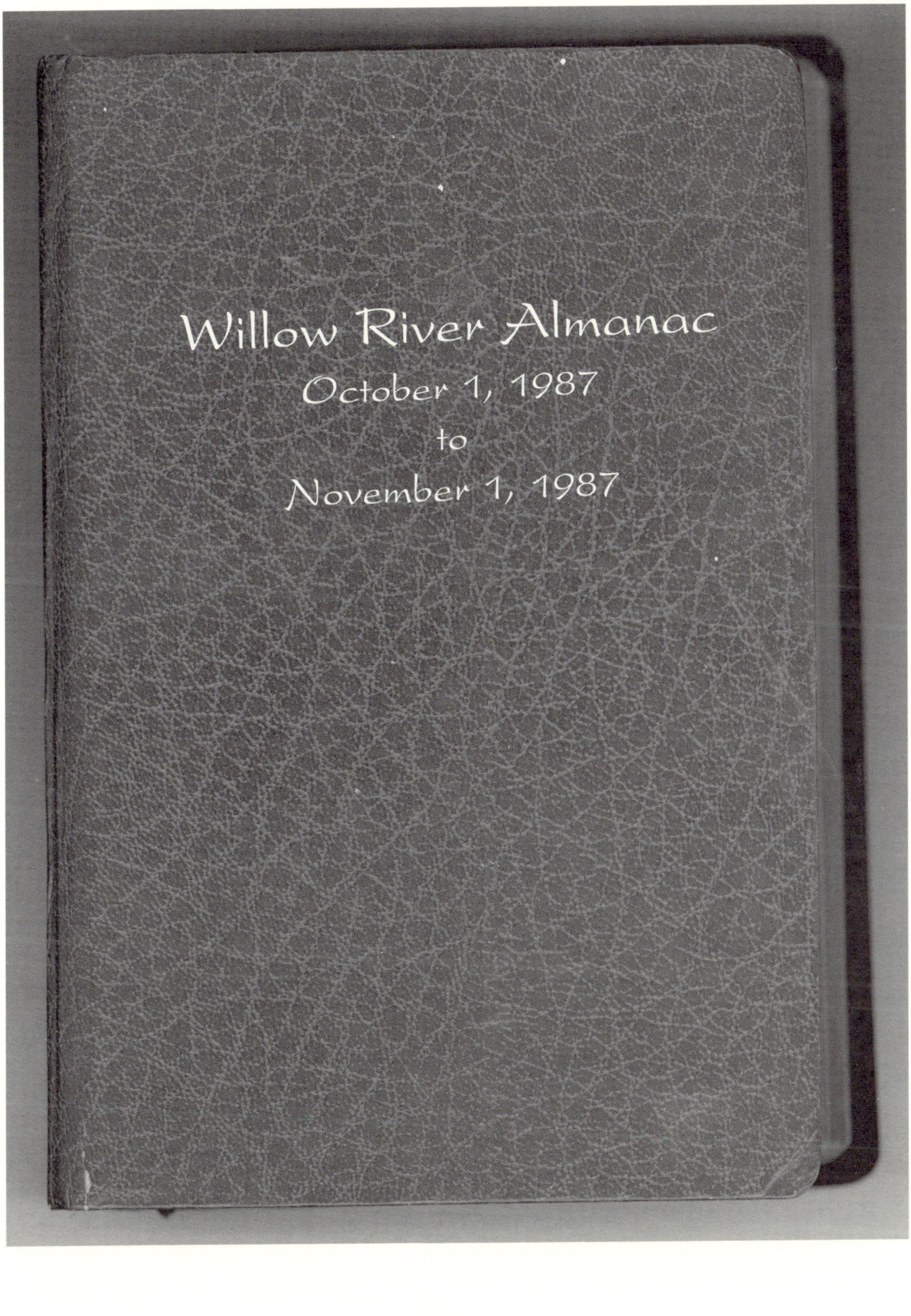
Willow River Almanac
October 1, 1987
to
November 1, 1987

1 Thursday

Willow River State Park is a 2,800-acre wonderland northeast of Hudson, and it offers a unique combination of woodland, water, and sprawling fields. Within the park boundaries are three lakes, three majestic (and that is no exaggeration) waterfalls, deep gorges, and steep overlooks.

The park entrance road winds through rolling hill and swale areas, and as I follow the meandering ribbon of highway, my eyes discover rounded, saucer-like depressions in the earth. These depressions were formed millions of years ago when great blocks of glacial ice became buried in glacial outwash material. When these submerged ice blocks melted, there were cave-ins from the ground above, which resulted in these rounded swale-like cavities.

My beloved poodle-terrier, Buttons, and I arrived at the park in the early hours of evening, just as the sun was disappearing behind the rounded hills and an artistic blend of bur and black oaks, aspen, paper birches, and black cherry trees. It was too dark to see beyond the shadows of the trees, and in my shattered emotional state, the forested carpetry looked almost foreboding.

I had not been out on my own for the past two decades, and when my writing endeavors had necessitated short journeys, there had always been a place to come home to. Now, like Sinclair Lewis, whom Thomas Wolfe had in mind in his novel, *You Can't Go Home Again,* there was no home, no welcoming arms, no smile of recognition—only a lonely, perhaps even ominous, unknown woodland.

As my 1985 Dodge van trudged involuntarily along the pavement that evening, I considered it almost amusing that I should be in a such a predicament, like the character in Robert Heinlein's science fiction novel, *A Stranger in a Strange Land.* Like Thomas Wolfe, I, too, had written a book based upon a Minnesota author who could never go home again, never dreaming, in a sense, that I was recording my autobiography. *Home at Last,* my second book, was still selling after six years, had been a Minnesota nonfiction bestseller once, if only for a solitary week, and was still earning me royalties.

I tried not to think of my four children—Stacy (sixteen), Stephanie (fourteen), John (eleven), and little Sarah (seven), but my mind was a battlefield, too numb to think of anything else. I wondered if they were thinking of me and where I might be, if I were safe or if they would ever see me again, as they coped with their communal pain in the house I once shared with them.

It had been difficult to cross the border into Wisconsin. Although I was only an hour away from those faces I loved dearly back in Minneapolis, it seemed light-years. I wanted to telephone, to write, to turn my van around and go running up those familiar steps, but like Sinclair Lewis, the fire I had ignited would never be snuffed out.

I had reached Willow River at dusk because I had spent the day attempting to gather the courage to leave Minnesota. When I had approached the St. Croix River, which separates Minnesota from Wisconsin, or that land where those dreadful Lilliputian Green Bay Packers dwelt, I exited and headed south on the Minnesota side. I had not gathered the strength I needed to cross that imaginary boundary, and I walked the daylight hours in Afton State Park.

I had hoped Afton would have a campground where I could park my van and be alone with my conscience, but the Minnesota park had none to offer. This meant, of course, I would have to cross the river and enter a land as foreign as the word "divorce." I think I knew the meaning of the forest, but it would be weeks before I really learned the true meaning of divorce.

The campground at Willow River was just what I had been looking for—wooded campsites that offered privacy, high above Little Falls Lake. I selected a campsite, number twenty-eight, because it seemed larger than the rest, offered more privacy than most, and presented a breath-taking view of the lake below.

Stepping out of my van, I let Buttons attempt to locate the ideal spot, which once may have been visited by another member of her breed. She did not like to urinate unless another dog had "broken in" the site before her. I peered through the darkness at what little of the lake I could see. A couple hundred feet from shore, I made out a canoe moving slowly along some Stygian "pathway," although the darkness prevented me from seeing its occupant.

I wondered what someone would be doing out on the lake after dark. The campground was only one-quarter full, and I had seen no one but a ranger since entering the park. The canoe, my only contact with humanity at the time, reminded me of the Boundary Waters Canoe Area of northern Minnesota, and the night and loneliness swept across my mind, recalling family vacations that were now only cobwebbed memories.

I lost sight of the canoe but ran along the shore, refusing to accept the reality that I had lost it in the night. I was alone! It recalled in my mind a period of twenty years earlier when I had been alone on the Kansas prairie, locked in a claustrophobic prison cell, straining to hear night sounds emanating from behind a stone wall. Then, too, I was lost and had felt an empty earth closing in on me, its civilization as dead as the cold planets beyond the asteroid belt.

Discovering a narrow trail leading into the woods, I walked a short distance, but the trail was rocky, and erosion had cut deep gouges in its surface, so I returned to the van. I was also afraid I would lose Buttons in the darkness. Faithful Buttons—my God—I couldn't have made it without her.

I never looked at a pet as being subject to me, and not once did I consider myself an owner of any living thing. Buttons was free to leave if she wanted, but I confess, I would have done everything possible to talk her out of it.

Buttons was more than just a friend or family pet. I had worked out a trade with my daughter Stacy the day I left my home and life behind and driven toward Willow River. I gave Stacy my twelve-inch portable television in exchange for Buttons, and she was worth every bit of it. Dogs, at least many of them, have a way of knowing when their human companion is down, and they, too, assume the same state of being.

So I wasn't alone. I had Buttons to share my misery.

When we returned to the van, I realized there wasn't anything to unpack, nothing to do but go to sleep in the back of the van. It was very cold; I had neglected to either bring along or purchase blankets, but I did have my sleeping bag.

I put on a thermal shirt, which served for pajamas and climbed into the bag. Still cold, I covered up with a bundle of clothes, and even used some of my seldom-worn suit coats as blankets. In the morning, I would just have to "dig" my way out of a mound of shirts, pants, jackets, and suit coats. The decision to use the clothing in such a fashion partially solved one problem but created another—I would run out of things to wear in a hurry.

There were high winds that night, and in them I could almost recognize voices calling out to me. This cacophony did not cease, and when the winds finally began to ebb, I immediately hungered for them to resume. I simply refused to let those night voices die, but, try as I might, the voices ceased calling me.

Tossing and turning, unable to sleep, my mind a fresh variety of roadkill somewhere back in Minneapolis, I strained for more sounds; anything similar to the wind songs that had kept me in touch with an imaginary humanity.

Sometime, shortly after midnight, I discerned a faint, shrill ticking that sounded somewhat like a home computer. At first, I thought I had imagined it, but the sound was repeated at regular intervals every few minutes. I had no idea where the sound originated. I was sure, however, it could not have emanated from a computer, but I was at a loss to recognize its source. I never did find out where the sound came from, and I never heard it again.

Over the years I had read scores of novels and short stories by British-born author Algernon Blackwood, including his supernatural classic, "The Wendigo." Many of Blackwood's tales were set in the remote wilderness of Canada, where he later lived, and the imaginary creature he built his story around was common folklore in the North Country.

While lying in the safety of my sleeping bag, stuffed in the back of my cold van, I remembered something my friend and fellow-writer Richard Tierney had once told me. Over a couple of summers, Tierney had served as a guide in the North Country of Minnesota along the Gunflint Trail, and one night, he and his party were awakened at their campsite on the edge of a lake by a faint noise, which neither crescendoed nor diminished. Tierney said the sound, far out across the water, sounded as if someone was holding down a piano key.

"I heard the Wendigo that night," Tierney, half in jest, had told me.

Richard L. Tierney is the only person I have ever known who has "heard" the Wendigo. As I listened to the shrill computer-like beeping, I wondered if someone else had just joined him in that coveted rank.

As torn apart as I was, I did not feel like laughing, but I think I did force a chuckle when I realized I had allowed a little night sound to try my imagination. As the faces of my children danced across my mind, and "the call of the Wendigo" soothed me into oblivion, I slept for what few hours remained of Day One at Willow River. In a few hours, I would see my first sunrise and more clearly what, for now, would be my new home.

2 Friday

As a child, I had been fond of birds and even considered myself some kind of amateur ornithologist. When I awoke with the sun on Day Two, I stepped from the van and gazed along the shore for killdeers, spotted sandpipers, common grackles, and kingfishers, which were said to be in abundance in the park. I was obviously no more than an amateur, for I had not considered the season.

But mesmerized, I looked around as though I were a tourist on vacation. My eyes scanned the far side of the water as I took in my first view of the lake by day.

I was surprised to discover, almost right next to me, a stairway leading down to the edge of the lake, and within minutes, I scurried down the wooden steps and stood on the shore of Little Falls Lake. Finding a not-too-uncomfortable spot to sit down, I sat in the sand and watched the waves slapping the shore. Far across the water, high atop a steep bluff, I glimpsed what looked like a castle, but which was in reality, a large, rustic, single-family home.

With Buttons at my heels, I climbed back up the stairs and followed a marker that led to the Willow Falls Trail. The trail lured me deep into the woods and around a curve, where I found myself walking along the bank of the Willow River. Not far from where the river emptied into Little Falls Lake, I observed a green, oozy coating of algae upon the water, although as I proceeded upstream, the river current was not so idle and the slime disappeared.

At one point along the trail, Buttons and I disturbed a conclave of crows who cawed obscenities at us and flew dive-bomb missions directly over our heads. The cawing birds followed us for about one hundred feet before the "warriors" returned to what they had been doing, and the only sound we heard was from the current of the river. Perhaps we had stumbled upon a feeding ground of the crows that saw tiny Buttons as a more dangerous adversary than myself.

Only then did I realize that I, too, should be eating, and I can honestly say, I hadn't thought about nutrition until that particular moment. I had been lost in a never-ending dream of my family and had not considered the rumblings in my stomach. The night winds had taught me to purchase blankets if I expected to stay warm at Willow River, and it took an attack of angry crows to remind me I was hungry.

At first, this stark realization frightened me because I knew the money I had could not last indefinitely. I still had close to $1,000, but with three meals a day, gas for the van, and blankets, pillows, and warm clothing, I could only hold out for a few weeks. I decided upon two meals a day instead of three.

I wondered what my wife and children were eating for breakfast back in Minneapolis, and I could picture the now-vacant chair at the east end of the table, which had for two decades been mine. I visualized those sad faces, all of them refusing to glance at the untenanted chair, all the while fighting my image in their minds.

Either a tear rolled down my cheek, or my face came too close to a spray mist from the river (I told myself it was the latter) when I saw those innocent family members putting more pancakes on their breakfast plates. They had done nothing to deserve this, neither had anyone else, but I blamed myself for being an alien monster who had allowed this to happen.

I knew I would never again sit in my designated chair—Dad's chair—and the image flashed across my mind like an old black-and-white movie that shows up night after night on late-night television. Willow River was now my home, and I would remain here until I could deal with my pain, even if it took forever.

At that particular moment, I realized I was conducting an experiment. I could not live in an apartment or down the block from people I had passed on the street every day. I needed the solitude and, if necessary, would live in the woods alone despite the nagging onslaught of winter. I would somehow learn to bask in my solitude and thumb my nose at the rest of the world.

Buttons and I were far from being alone on the winding trail, for a multitude of chipmunks or gophers, squirrels, rabbits, "friendly" snakes, and an occasional deer joined us on our trek. I found the chipmunks incredibly interesting, if that is what they were, for I have never known the difference between a chipmunk and a gopher.

Minnesota has an abundance of gophers—it is even nicknamed the Gopher State—and these Wisconsin varieties looked no different from the thousands I had seen back home. One came so close, I nearly managed to touch it. I counted thirteen stripes and called it a "thirteen-stripe gopher" before Buttons mounted her courage and chased it away.

We saw no people on the trail, but I wasn't surprised, since the campground had been virtually empty that morning. The roaring of the river increased, and it became quite apparent that we were approaching a series of rapids or, perhaps, a waterfall. The bank between the river and us grew much steeper, and I was a little concerned Buttons would plunge over the edge.

Buttons must have been thinking the same and had not been paying attention to where she was stepping, for I saw her suddenly leap straight into the air. She had inadvertently stepped on a slithering garter snake, which hastily retreated into the brush. Buttons turned predator and gave pursuit, but the victimized viper outfoxed her.

The black-and-yellow-green-striped garter snake is only one of a variety of constrictors in the park, none of which are poisonous. Fox snakes, yellow-tan with large brown blotches on their bodies, are also fairly common. The fox snake, with its penny-colored head, will frequently coil like a rattler, but it is harmless.

The park also claims small green snakes, tiny light brown snakes with pink bellies called brown snakes, and a tiny cousin with a brick-red belly called a red-bellied snake. Perhaps the most terrifying snake at Willow River is the hog-nosed snake, which is occasionally glimpsed in the open fields. The heavy-set, brownish-blotched hog-nose, if threatened, has a habit of flattening its head like a cobra and hissing. Like the others, however, it is non-poisonous.

I was meeting my neighbors, and I soon realized they slithered and hissed no differently than many people I had

known back in the city. Of course, Buttons had just made a bad impression on one of the local residents, but it was fun to watch her play bully as if she thought she was protecting me.

Before I could force a chuckle, I gazed upon a site so breath-taking, it was difficult to imagine it anywhere but in one of our national parks in the American West. Above me loomed a scenic gorge, and from the top of the Willow Falls Dam, water gushed 101 feet to the river below.

It was undoubtedly one of the most picturesque waterfalls I had ever seen, and of course, my wife had the camera, along with everything else, back in Minneapolis. I later learned the sixty-four-foot-wide waterfalls backed up the ninety-one-acre Burkhardt's Millpond. This dam featured four twelve-foot gates, opened and closed by park officials, to control the level of the lake downriver.

My thoughts drifted to my wife, my beloved companion of so many years, and to hundreds of vacation treasures just like this falls that we had driven thousands of miles to see together. I was hurt because I knew this was one vista she would never see with me. I was sad because she would never see this gorge, but I suffered all the more knowing I would be robbed of the enjoyment of sharing her reaction to its beauty.

Just then, I considered this sacred waterfall in Willow River one of the most magnificent sites I would ever see. This wasn't necessarily a positive sensation, because the reality of it was I was seeing it alone. Those rugged cliffs, the cascading of laughing water, only amplified my loneliness. The beautiful face of my wife became superimposed over the falls—beauty complimenting beauty—but what good was beauty when no other eyes were there to behold it?

I turned my back on the falls, and in doing so, on reality as well. I backtracked a few hundred feet and followed another path up a steep incline. I found the hill so steep, I had to rest several times during the ascent. Buttons, too, had trouble negotiating the climb, but I picked up all nine-and-one-half pounds of her. Still, carrying a dog of even slight proportion, was no easy task.

We once stopped beside a paper birch tree, whose silvery-white bark is easily peeled, which is why the Indians used it to make their canoes. Like birch bark, I, too, was coming apart as I climbed to the top of the hill. If I could continue moving, I thought that perhaps I could prevent my feelings from catching up with me.

As Buttons and I trudged along a new trail atop the bluff and headed back in the direction of our campsite, we discovered some head stones that marked the graves of a pioneer family near a rugged but pulchritudinous overlook. It was apparent from another marker, which indicated the site of their homestead, that this William Scott family had come to Willow River prior to the Civil War. I was determined to ask a ranger about the Scotts as soon as the opportunity presented itself.

The upper trail provided many scenic vistas but I preferred the lower trail I had walked since it was much more isolated.

By the time we found our way back to the van, I realized we had not met a single person on any of the trails. I was glad. I certainly did not feel like talking with anyone, unless it was a ranger who might be able to answer some of my questions.

I was lonely, but I was also hungry. I decided to drive into Hudson to pick up some food and miscellaneous supplies. I stopped at the park entrance and asked the ranger on duty about William Scott.

Scott, I learned, was the first white settler in the Willow River area. He came to Hudson with his sons from what is now St. Stephens, New Brunswick. In Canada, they had lived along a river called the St. Croix and decided to move to Wisconsin because there was also a St. Croix River there.

In 1849, the Scotts traveled by boat down the Erie Canal, then rode a stagecoach to Lakeland, Minnesota, just across the St. Croix from Hudson. Borrowing a rowboat, they rowed across the river to Wisconsin in search of an ideal location to build a house.

Discovering Willow River Falls, the men climbed the steep bank, and decided to build on the rich prairie land above where they could appreciate the impressive river beauty below.

Scott received the first land grant to farm the Hudson prairie and had his home completed by 1850. He eventually moved his family there.

After enjoying my first meal since I had come to Wisconsin, I stopped in a small department store and purchased the cheapest blanket I could find. The blanket, which cost but seven dollars, would keep some of the chill out, but it was only as thick as a daily newspaper. I should have purchased a better blanket of real wool, but I was budgeting, and it was the best I could do.

In addition to the blanket, I bought a towel, washrag, a can opener, loaf of bread, jar of peanut butter, soft drinks, several cans of beans (which I could cook right in the can), and dog food. Before returning to Willow River, I drove to the top of the bluff in Hudson's Birkmose Park, walked along the Indian mounds, and took in the view of the St. Croix Valley.

I was kidding myself and I knew it. I was really looking at Minnesota across the St. Croix. I longed to see it, needed to know it was still there, so by some chance, maybe one day I could go back to my home and all would be forgotten. Just maybe . . . .

We returned to the park at sunset and glimpsed several deer on the road to the campground. I walked around the campground and marveled at the sunset over the lake as if it were part of a beautiful painting. The air had grown quite cool, and the crackling fires of the few hardy campers who had stayed on here hissed and spat and gave birth to writhing shadows along the wall of trees.

I felt as though I had stepped into a Currier & Ives greeting card. The scent of cooked meat brought me back many years to a campground high atop Mt. Ranier in Washington State. I had been with my wife and children on a family vacation, and on our way to the summit at Paradise Point, we stopped for a cookout. God, if I could only go back. I would do anything. Anything! The image passed quickly.

After dark, I had a major moving job in the back of the van, refolding all the clothing, which had served as blankets, before snuggling into my sleeping bag for the night. With my "newspaper" of a blanket, it was cold—twenty-eight degrees—and Buttons crawled into the bottom of the bag and slept between my feet. I was afraid she would suffocate because little air found its way inside. She must have known what she was doing, however, and never complained.

I could not sleep initially and would sit up every time a car drove through the campground. The headlights from the incoming automobiles played tricks on me by illuminating what appeared to be a road sign just to the right of my site. I had not recalled seeing any such sign, but the lights of each car caused it to glow.

As I lay awake, I wondered what might transpire if, in the morning, I were to drive across the river, telephone my son, and ask him to get permission to join me at Willow River for the weekend. I could make it alone, I reasoned, because I just had to be away from all the turmoil, but if I could just see one of the kids . . . .

3 Saturday

When I awakened in the early hours of morning, I looked about for the ghostly sign but found nothing. It was quite apparent, however, a reflection from the silvery-white bark of a paper birch was the culprit. I enjoyed a "hearty" breakfast of bread, peanut butter, and diet cola and planned my day.

Leaving the park, I drove to Hudson, crossed the St. Croix River, and pulled into a rest area on the Minnesota side. Following a quick telephone call to my eighty-year-old uncle, "Dodo," I drove to St. Paul and on into Minneapolis. I was picking him up and bringing him back for a one-day tour of Willow River.

Dodo is not really my uncle, and Dodo is only a nick-name. His real name is Joe Wise, and he was my late father's best friend. As kids, my brother (also deceased) and I could not pronounce "Joe" and substituted "Dodo," thinking we had said it correctly. Joe became Dodo, and Dodo became almost a third parent to me as well as my best friend. If anyone understood me, certainly he did.

Dodo had always been a camera buff and connoisseur of scenic parkland, and he was more than anxious to see my new home. I told him I considered Willow River my home, I had accepted my dismal plight, and had decided to stay on regardless of winter. I would require at least a month in the woods to get my head back on straight. I was sure it would be awhile before I could interact with other people again. Of course, Dodo wasn't people; he was family.

The rolling hills, rugged-looking forests and majestic waterways immediately impressed him. When we reached the campground on the south shore of Little Falls Lake, he was out of the van before me, anxious to explore the expanse on foot. I cautioned him about taking it easy. He was, after all, eighty years old, but it had never stopped him before and would not hinder him today.

As Dodo, Buttons, and I set off through the pristine forest along the Willow Falls Trail, I almost felt good again for the first time in a week. I was no longer alone, and as we walked and talked, I told Dodo everything regarding the separation and pending divorce.

At first, he questioned my living in the woods as a means of combating the pain of a marriage and broken lives. After all, he rationalized, I could move in with him and his wife or other family members and friends temporarily. I told him he would understand once he had seen my woods. He was well aware of my quest for solitude, and although he was concerned about my safety, he admitted some miles up the trail, the quiet woodland was, perhaps, the best place for me just then.

Dodo snapped nearly an entire roll of film at Willow Falls, and as we leaned from the railing at the observation overlook, the mist dancing playfully off our faces, I thought I would never get him away from there. But I didn't mind waiting; I had suddenly gone back to the cherished 1940s and '50s of my childhood all over again.

A fish jumped beneath us, but it happened so quickly, neither of us caught more than a glimpse, and we could not identify it. I remembered some of the fishing trips when, as a kid, Dodo had taken me to Lake Minnetonka to catch sunfish, crappie, and bass. I had always wanted to catch a pickerel after seeing a picture of one, but to this day, I don't think I have ever seen one.

For the first time in over a week, I laughed out loud, for, recalling those fishing trips, I also remembered Dodo as a victim of my negligence. As a youngster, I had accidentally knocked his rod and reel into the water, tangled my line in a tree, propelled my hook into his skin just below the eye, let a whole day's catch of fish get away, laughed when the fish he was removing from my hook nearly peed in his face, and told the streetcar conductor I was six when he had instructed me to insist I was five.

My wandering mind returned to Willow River and Dodo, who was still standing there, mesmerized by the roaring river. I felt a tear trickle from my eye as I watched him. I think this was the first time I could see him slowly getting old before me. He had always been a part of my life, and the thought of his not being there one day caused me to turn my face away from him to hide my expression.

When my brother, Bobby, had been killed in a pre-Christmas auto accident in 1960, it was Dodo who rallied my mother, father, and me together, with warm words and an understanding heart. I was too selfish then to be aware that behind his mask, Dodo was crying too.

When I was called home from the Kansas prairie in 1967 following the death of my father, it was Dodo who accompanied my mother and future wife to the airport to receive me. Dodo had seemed so strong, so fearless, and as before, his support served as an inspiration. I now wonder how many nights when he was alone, he cried too.

Hell, he had even been there when a motorist had killed my dog. I was a little kid when we sat on the steps of a neighborhood business and surveyed busy Riverside Avenue, where the hit-and-run incident had taken place. Dodo could not keep me from crying that dismal night in 1953, but when I peeked between my fingers, I learned then that grownups also cried.

Dodo's words, "I want to see more of this place," jarred me from my stupor, and nodding my head, my eyes not yet dry, we marched back along the trail. When we reached the cross trail that led up the steep hill, I turned away from it and started walking the way we had come.

"Where you going?" Dodo asked, as if I had committed a sin. "I want to climb this hill and get a view of Willow River from the top."

"Jesus," I snapped. "You are eighty years old. I had all I could do to make it to the top."

He insisted upon climbing the hill with or without me and began the arduous climb, which constituted the steepest trail in the park. Between quarter and halfway, I think he realized he had erred but was too stubborn to turn back. We paused to rest at least a half dozen times, and he admitted I had been right.

I wanted to help him with the climb, but he shrugged off any assistance.

"I'm not as ancient a critter as you think," he barked.

When we finally reached the top, we both were winded and sat down for a rest on a bench. The view was spectacular, and I remarked to Dodo the river valley was nothing short of "pulchritudinous." Dodo laughed, for he remembered when as a kid, I had seen the word in a Superman comic book and had looked up its meaning to impress him with my vocabulary.

It was a cool day, but on top of the bluffs, the sun was shining to make our walk a pleasant one. When we reached the homestead and graves of the Scott family, I delivered a short oral history, as I followed him about while he took another wave of pictures.

When we found our way back to the campground, we were both very tired. Getting into the van, I drove us to the boat launch area, which afforded a good view of the lake.

Walking along the beach, I showed him an amphitheater where rangers conduct field-trip talks during the summer months. The open area seemed lonely because I could not visualize real people being there.

Dodo was very impressed by the Lower or Little Falls Dam with its controlling gates and a spillway from Little Falls Lake. He took many photographs of the dam and 158-acre lake that backed up behind it before we left the park. I drove him home to Minneapolis in the afternoon.

I felt sorry for myself after letting Dodo off and turning onto Lake Street. I became cognizant that in the lonely, remote woods of Willow River, I had been at peace, but suddenly back in the city where I had lived all my life, I was now an outsider, an alien or nonentity. I wondered if Thoreau had felt this way at Walden Pond, or August Derleth when he had gone to his railroad trestle in the swamp along the Wisconsin River to get away and write.

I took from under my seat what I considered my Bible—Henry Beston's *The Outermost House*, which he had written to chronicle a solitary year on a Cape Cod beach. Beston had scribbled the book in longhand at a kitchen table in a little room with windows overlooking the North Atlantic and the dunes.

At that moment, I knew my own diary, incoherent as it was, was shaping into a book. My previous books had involved years of research, but this one would not. To this book, I needed no interviews, no reference notes, no bibliography. I only needed to give it my heart.

I recalled one of my favorite passages from *The Outermost House* about a bird called an aukie that Beston found fluttering along the beach, its wings covered with a sticky fuel oil. I remembered Beston's words because they had so moved me: "Strange little fragment of life on the edge of that mysterious immensity." I, too, was a fragment of life, shattered by the impending divorce, for what little remained of my emotional stability had left me something less than whole. Beston, however, had done his best to nurse the aukie back to health, and I realized Willow River was my tonic. I, too, would one day "fly" away. Still there seemed little hope for me. A broken wing is much different from a broken heart.

Although I may not have fully comprehended his meaning, Beston wrote two passages that helped me understand my plight and started me thinking of my situation.

"Nature is part of our humanity, and without some awareness and experience of that divine mystery, man ceases to be man."

Could I solve nature's mystery? If I could only grasp the meaning of the Master Plan, I could better accept my role in my own struggle.

Beston also penned, "Man can either be less than man or more than man, and both are monsters, the last more dread."

Maybe I was not so unique in this world of monsters. There were several others fighting a losing battle, and many of them were much more unfortunate. Maybe Stacy, Stephanie, John, and Sarah would understand their father as something less than perfection. Perhaps, I hoped, they wanted to see me as much as I wanted to see them.

Before going to a public telephone, I reached under the seat and removed some letters sent me by John and little Sarah, which Dodo had hand-carried to me. I find it difficult to dwell on the letters (which I may always carry) for I honestly cannot look at them without crying. I may be able to confront them one day, long after they are dirt-stained and tattered, very much like my heart is just now.

My children conveyed their love to me, and I longed to see them even more as I held those letters in my hand. I was afraid to look at them a second time in case I had read them wrong or they had been only part of a dream. One line in Sarah's letter had really got me: "I will never forget you, Dad," and as I recalled those pitiful words, I began to cry.

I suppose there are fathers who deserve to be called jerks during and following a divorce, and many deserve everything they get (or don't get). Being cast out from a family—right, wrong or indifferent—automatically shapes that parent as "the bad guy." Of course, the absenteeism adds to the tar-

nished image. But I wonder—Oh God, how I wonder—how many wives, good and bad, really understand a father's pain, let alone, a father's love. Sometimes children are able to understand it better.

My telephone call found John just home from school, and I was elated when he said he wanted to spend the weekend with me at Willow River. After procuring permission from his mother, I picked up John, along with our family dog Cassie, a Dalmation, and headed back along I-94 toward Wisconsin.

John and I talked very little during the ride. I am sure he did not know how to say what was in his heart, and the lump in my throat prevented any interchange on my part. He did tell me Cassie had missed me very much, which was evident by the way she had jumped all over me. And she was even more excited to see Buttons, and vice versa, and for one whole weekend, Buttons could play "Follow-the-Leader-Pee-pee."

After sandwiches in Hudson, we entered Willow River State Park late in the evening, both of us beginning to talk, but neither of us discussing the break-up. We went to bed—John on the car seat, me on the floor—but neither of us could sleep.

John jumped up several times. Whenever a car entered the campground, I pointed out the "ghost sign," and he tried to guess what it was. He laughed when I told him it would not be there in the morning when we awoke.

The night was cool but not necessarily cold. Since we could not sleep, we took the dogs on a short night hike up the Willow Falls Trail. We could not venture far because of the darkness, but it was rewarding to have the dogs reunited and trotting happily together, with John at my side.

I think we re-established, to a small degree, our relationship that night. We had not discussed anything pertinent to the family break-up, and we certainly concealed our individual pain, but a bond, which could never be completely broken, remained and strengthened between us.

Just before we fell asleep, someone in the campground set ablaze a mad flurry of bottle rockets, which lit up the night sky with a shower of flashing colors. It was like the Fourth of

July, but far stranger, because there were so few campers left in the campground. I felt as if the fireworks display had been performed for our own benefit, and, almost believing this, I really did not want to know who had set them off.

I looked at John—my son, so much a part of me—with tears in my eyes, but with tears of joy, for, albeit briefly, we were once more together. We had "oohed" and "awed" over the cavalcade of lights, and when I went to sleep, I felt good again. I slept soundly that night, for the first time since coming to Willow River.

4 Sunday

A wilderness area such as Willow River belongs to no individual but is for everyone to share and enjoy. My house, family, land, and everything I cherished back in the city no longer belonged to me either. I had learned to realize daily struggles in the structured family were not unlike those encountered in the wilderness. Bonds forged by pen and paper could vanish as quickly as animal tracks in the forest. My marriage contract had been issued as well as terminated much in the same manner as the campground permit I had paid for and would one day surrender. Sadly, there is always an expiration date.

People who cared had protected me in the city, and, blessed with four walls, three meals, and a routine, I seldom needed to go beyond my element. I had never dreamed my serenity could be punctured, then shattered. Instability, I would have thought, was out of the question.

When dreams came suddenly to an end, a bond was broken, followed by my heart and, undoubtedly, my mind. How could I ever be expected to live in some apartment on a foreign street and attempt to disguise my pain from the nameless faces with which I would be forced to interact upon a daily basis?

I felt I had made the right decision by coming to Willow River. I had come to hide my pain and get my head back on straight, so one day I could return to the outside world.

I was not prepared to meet the world this morning as John and I descended the steep stairway to the lake below, with Cassie taking three steps at a time and little Buttons negotiating each one slowly and meticulously. I was not sure I was ready to talk with John yet, for he was having a good time, and I did not want to say or do anything that might threaten his state of being, or for that matter, my own.

John, who had brought fishing gear, wanted to see the lake close-up. He was a fisherman at heart, and although I had seldom taken him, he had fished many times with his uncle Phil. We sat on a rock on the shore of the lake, and John asked if I would talk to the ranger regarding fishing regulations for children. I told him I would.

We left the lake, postponed any further talk of fishing, and set off on a morning exercise trek along the Willow Falls Trail. There are many trails in the park but this particular one was my favorite.

The dogs raced far ahead and reached the bend where the trail stretches its elbow and follows the river. Buttons was thrilled in being reunited with Cassie, and Cassie was in her glory just being one of the gang. The dogs paused several times to investigate animal droppings and sniffed the air for more pleasant scents.

The river on our left ran swiftly this morning, and the gurgling sound set a rapid cadence for our march. We didn't talk very much; we didn't have to. The morning was brisk, and it was just nice to be out enjoying it.

The falls, which flowed from Burkhardt Millpond, were always beautiful, and this morning was no exception. I had learned from a ranger that the steep walls of the gorge are composed of Prairie du Chien limestone deposited over 400 million years ago by the Ordovician Sea.

The bank below the cascading water was a good place to rest. I found it difficult to pull myself away from the cataract, and, when we departed, we did so gazing over our shoulders. When we reached the dreaded hill, we climbed without resting, although I cheated just a little.

On the upper prairie, we veered from the direction of the Scott homestead and followed a narrow path to the ranger station near the entrance of the park. I asked the ranger on duty about the possibility of my son fishing and was delighted in learning my youngster needed no license.

According to the ranger and a little tabloid newspaper he gave me, such was not always the case along Willow River. In 1896, a group calling itself the Willow River Club purchased 200 acres along the river and attempted to prevent non-members from fishing on their land. Frank Wade, a Civil War veteran, logger, and avid trout fisherman, contested the city's claim because the Willow was a navigable river. He was arrested for fishing on the river.

In 1898, the Wisconsin State Supreme Court acted in Wade's favor, declaring the Willow a navigable stream in which no club could halt fishing activity. Because of Frank Wade's fight eighty-nine years earlier, my son was fishing the Willow before the day was over.

While talking to the ranger, I solved the mystery of what I had called a "thirteen-stripe chipmunk," which in reality is a thirteen-lined ground squirrel or gopher. There are also pocket gophers in the park, although many move about primarily after dark. On the way to the ranger station, however, we did "stumble" upon their freshly dug earth mounds, many of which reached four to five inches in height and were up to a foot in diameter.

From the ranger station, we followed another narrow trail skirting the Scott homesite and headed back to the campground via the Bur Oak Nature Trail. Along this trail there was but a single conifer—a red cedar—although the entire area might have been tree-covered in the distant past.

One did not have to be a botanist to realize the aspen trees were invading the grasslands here. These trees taper from taller to shorter, older to younger, as they advance into the field like a conquering army. Ecologists call this advancement, "plant succession," and, as the process continues, oak trees will eventually follow suit.

As we hiked the trail, we saw a couple of sapling trees, plus gray dogwood, blackberry, smooth sumac, American hazelnut, and scores of young oak trees. One day the trees will take over, shade the scrubs, and reduce their number.

I could not help thinking of the ever-changing typography and how a change in nature paralleled the sudden change in my own life. Human life, like nature, is not a constant, but a series of changes, good and bad. What a pity that we cannot foresee these changes in our lives, as we can predict inevitable alterations in nature. Of course, I said nothing to John about any of this; his mind was far away on fishing.

Interpretive markers posted along the trail described the wildlife. Many mammals visit the Bur Oak, among them weasels, fox, deer-mice, rabbits, and white-tailed deer. Birds, too, are frequent visitors, and those commonly glimpsed are catbirds, brown thrashers, towhees, cardinals, and grouse.

Many resident birds make their homes along or near the trail; most commonly the black-capped chickadees, white-breasted nuthatch, cardinals, blue jays, both hairy and downy woodpeckers, crows, ruffed grouse, and the great horned owl. Summer visitors include the Baltimore oriole, wood pewee, red-eyed vireo, scarlet tanager, rose-breasted grosbeak, redstart, indigo bunting, robin, and wood thrush.

Most of the birds along the Bur Oak live in harmony although the rarely seen, but occasionally present, cooper's hawk and sharp-shinned hawk disrupt the community. If any hawks were in the area, John and I did not see them.

On our right, we could see the Willow River Valley below and could almost pick out the trail where we had entered the forest. The long, high ridge above the river, called a terminal moraine, was formed when the last glacier covered the valley.

During our trek, we saw many bracken or "three-parted" ferns clustered around several species of heavy, strong-wooded oak trees, including the northern pine oak and the white oak. Gray dogwood trees dotted the trail, as did an abundance of basswood trees or American linden.

I could easily picture local Indians using the outer basswood bark to cover their wigwams and weaving the tough, fibrous inner bark into ropes and mats. From the soft, pliable wood of the basswood, they fashioned bowls from which they ate their meals.

Long before these Indians roamed the valley, the entire Willow River area was covered by a layer of glacial sand, gravel, and boulders collectively called "glacial drift." Much of this material had been "picked up" in Canada and had become trapped in the thick ice of the Wisconsin glacier, which covered the park for tens of thousands of years. The glacier slowly melted only ten to fifteen thousand years ago and deposited its load of sand and rocks on top of the area.

When the thick glacial sand blanket was initially deposited, the land's surface was nearly flat, and the broad, picturesque Willow River Valley 15,000 years ago was non-existent. Sand was easily moved by running water and the young river selected its course on this new sand blanket.

A down-cutting, widening process still continues. Whenever water runs down the dry creek bed, the little valley widens, although plant roots, dead leaves, and branches delay the erosion process.

John did his best to rush me through the nature area, and I nearly chuckled out loud when I considered it had taken a glacier, and the efforts of Frank Wade, to make possible the fishing he was hurrying to enjoy. I did not share his enthusiasm and told him so. Why would anyone ever want to leave an Eden like the Bur Oak Nature Trail? Only John knew.

We gaped at prickly ash trees along the trail, which are related to orange trees and other citrus plants. Their leaves have a strong lemon scent, and when I paused and sniffed their heavy fragrance, I was reminded of the delicious lemonade my father used to make when I was a child.

Both Indians and early white pioneers once chewed the bark of the ash trees to soothe painful toothaches. If I should suffer the same malady and run out of money, I'd probably have to resort to chewing this bark myself.

Not only humans find the ash tree useful. I read that giant swallowtail butterflies, when in their caterpillar stage, eat the leaves. Since the prickly ash is the only "plant" in

Wisconsin whose leaves the caterpillars eat, we would never see the insect if not for the trees.

I did not tarry, for John reminded me of my promise to walk a wee bit faster.

As we wound our way through the grove, I could see the bur oak was king here. The insulating bark makes the bur oak Wisconsin's most fire-resistant tree. We also passed several hackberry trees, boxelders, American elms, and hophornbeam trees, which are related to European hornbean trees once used to make ox yokes.

As we entered the canyon along the lower part of the trail, we came upon several "interrupted" ferns. These ferns were thusly named because the fertile fronds of the species have dark brown spore masses interrupting their fronds. They are especially dense and large in the cool, wooded ravines and dark valleys which comprise the canyon. It was easy to picture ourselves in a science fiction movie where nature had gone wild, or in the pages of H. G. Wells' novel, *The Food of the Gods*, for some of the fronds were nearly five feet long.

We also saw maidenhair ferns and sarsaparilla ferns with slender, shiny, black stems and delicate circular fronds. In what I termed, "The Valley of Ferns," we discovered some spinulose woodferns and a few lady ferns. The lady ferns are a lighter green than most of their cousins and not so sharply toothed on the margins of their leaflets.

The maidenhair and sarsaparilla ferns were more familiar to me than the others, but I have read there are 7,227 recognized species of ferns throughout the world.

About 200 million years ago, these ferns were the size of trees and grew into vast jungles. These ancient fern forests evolved into our present-day coal beds. Sarsaparilla plants are used to make root beer.

Before leaving the Bur Oak, where it merged with one of the trails in the valley, we saw the autumnal remains of a wild strawberry patch. The matted greenery stretched along both sides of the pathway.

American Indians once picked strawberries long before the coming of the white man, as did bear and smaller animals.

Many people consider strawberries nature's best berry. Naturalist William Butler once said of wild strawberries: "Doubtless God could have made a better berry, but doubtless, God never did."

I wished there had been berries.

As we descended the gully that lead to the campground, I slipped on a rock and fell flat on my posterior. The fall was nothing unique, for in actuality, I had fallen three successive days while hiking. The result of this third fall, however, was a bit more painful, as I aggravated an old ankle injury and had to be helped back to camp by John.

After preparing and eating a small lunch, I found I still could not walk without pain. The ankle had swollen and the pain had increased. With a noticeable limp I could get around, but the more I hobbled, the more the pain increased. I did not recall anything like this happening to Thoreau at Walden Pond.

John descended the high stairway in the rear of our campground, rod and reel in hand. Not wishing to hurt my ankle more than I already had, I sat on top of the stairway and watched him fish for crappies. The ranger had told him to use white jigs for lures, and although he followed the advice, he came up empty-handed. A little frustrated, he removed a jig and tried his luck with buzz bait, again with no results.

When he returned to Site Twenty-Eight, we drove over to the playground, and I sat in the van while he frolicked. The respite was brief, however, for fishing still occupied his mind. We drove over to the boat launch area where he tried fishing from the rocks.

As he tried his luck again, I sat with the dogs at the empty amphitheater and contemplated my very real situation. I felt very close to John, and I think that day, we came to respect each other a little more than before. We were father and son, different in many ways but enjoying a common experience. John knew his father was a writer and considered a bit of a rebel and at times even odd, but he accepted this without question. I wished my wife, more mature but less caring, could feel the same way he did.

After all, I knew my son had fishing in his blood. I admired him for pursuing his interest, and although I cared nothing about fishing, I did all I could to show my love by being with him.

We were not at the lake long when John bagged his first crappie, followed by another and another. He fished for sport, not for supper, and I respected him for his catch-and-release ethics. He knew we would not be cooking fish, so he was more than glad to let them go.

John decided to try his luck at the Little Falls Dam, near the controlling gates and spillway where the ranger had said the "big ones" leaped. As we walked (he walked, I stumbled) out onto the dam and he began fishing, we watched a fisherman below us on the bank pulling in one crappie after another.

While John was obsessed with duplicating the fisherman's feat, I was awe-struck by the north wall of the gorge below the dam with its thick-layered sandstone. According to geologists, this Cambrian sandstone was deposited on the bottom of the Cambrian Sea, which covered most of Wisconsin over 500 million years ago.

To John's delight, the fisherman below the dam must have caught his limit, for he gathered his equipment and marched back towards the parking lot. John reacted instantly and assumed his former rival's position along the bank. Receiving no nibbles in the first few minutes, he improvised a bit and sidestepped several feet and again tried his luck.

During one of his casts, his rubber hook became imbedded in a fallen tree, and in spite of my warning shouts, he waded into the water and attempted to free it. Finally heeding my warnings, he returned to the bank, his line still tangled miserably in the branches over the water. Although my ankle was throbbing, but not nearly as severely as before, I climbed out on the tree over the river and shook the line free. John's smile of gratitude was all I needed to forget whatever pain still remained in my ankle.

John did manage to haul in and release a few crappies, and after he had fished his fill, we walked a short distance down the Little Falls Trail.

The Little Falls Trail is one of the longest trails in the park, meandering from the beach through a forest, to the park office where it parallels the forest edge. It ends in a very steep hill leading down to Willow Falls Dam.

There are markers on most of the trails at Willow River, which indicate on maps both the course and length of the walkways. It was very obvious to me that any real exploration on our part would require a little stamina. Because we had walked so much already, and my ankle was not in shape for such an expedition, we postponed the full trek for another time.

The Trout Brook Trail, which begins in the same general area, was a much easier hike with its level surface. The trail wanders along the Lower Willow trout stream and is a bird watcher's delight, even in the fall. But darkness was descending, so we decided to conduct a more thorough investigation later.

When we reached the van, I discovered a wood tick on John, and shortly after removing it, located one of its relatives clinging to myself. A further search turned up another tick on Cassie. Buttons had the distinction of being the only member of our party to be declared tickless.

I hated the drive back to Minneapolis, for I knew once I dropped off John and Cassie, it would be another week before I could enjoy company again. My son loathed the parting too, and I took comfort in his pledge that he'd come back to Willow River next weekend, once the school week was over.

Buttons and I returned to Willow River after 10:00 P.M., "anchored" the van safely in Site #28, and walked through the deserted campground, guided by the ever-weakening ray of my battery-operated flashlight. Only three other sites were occupied, a sure indication winter was on its way. With John gone, I was lonelier than before, and the emotional pain of separation nearly drove me to tears.

Willow River was now a dead place and an empty one. Those sacred spots John and I had walked together but a few hours earlier were forlorn and wanting, and I shunned them. This denial was so impossible, so difficult. The places my son and I had shared loomed all around me, bigger and blacker than ever before. Yet, I was grateful for the darkness, which concealed those familiar sites from my eyes.

Two middle-aged ladies from one of the campsites passed Buttons and me in the dark, and I could tell they were frightened of us. As they marched to the bathrooms and into the sanctuary of light, they continued to glance over their shoulders, making sure we were not following.

I retired at midnight. I do not know which was worse, the aching in my ankle or the pain in my heart. I wanted my son back, my three daughters, my entire family. I thought I could endure the terrible loneliness, the pain of exile, but I was near giving up just then. Maybe I could just walk into the woods, into the water maybe, and never, ever have to struggle with my loneliness again. I thought of my family in Minneapolis—their conversations, their laughter, and their security in being together. There is strength in numbers. A tiny dog and me! But, we would go on somehow.

As Buttons burrowed into my sleeping bag, I became aware of the weather, but for the first time since coming to Willow River, I did not let the cold bother me. Previous nights had seemed colder, but I knew we would wake up freezing in the early hours of morning.

5 Monday

A pounding rain disturbed my sleep some time before dawn, and as I listened to the incessant drumming on the roof of the van, I remembered a small leakage problem in the back doors. Climbing to the back of the van in the semi-darkness, I found nothing wet, but as a precaution rearranged my baggage, and stuffed several paper napkins as reinforcement of the "dike" between the doors before returning to my sleeping bag.

Funny how we take the warmth of a house for granted. All my life I had slept at home, comfortable, seldom thinking of others outside in need of sanctuary. I had never dreamed something as simple as rain would become a factor in my self-preservation. For that matter, I had never been concerned with self-preservation in my life, save for that year in prison, and I was not prepared for even this little emergency. In only a matter of days I had forced myself to adapt to the ways of the wild, but the learning process was far from over.

I was now used to the chilling air of Willow River, to being cold and alone, and to taking advantage of any warmth I might be blessed with, regardless of its brief duration. As I turned the engine on to get the chill out of the air, Buttons burrowed deeper into my sleeping bag, and I realized she, too, was making the best of it.

Changing into a warmer "nightshirt," my hand brushed my cheek. I was shocked to discover the cracked and wind-burned condition of my skin. I wanted to laugh, then cry, over the turtle-like texture, which in just a few days, had become tough as leather. I suppose the transformation was necessary and the epidermal metamorphosis would continue as the weather turned colder.

I felt I had gained weight. I had been eating one meal a day in Hudson and two at my campsite. Yes, I had promised myself I would eat but two meals a day, but the plan had not yet gone into operation. Still, I would have thought an unsteady diet and walking about ten miles a day would have produced the opposite effect. But I definitely felt heavier.

I was no longer taking warmth for granted as I had done in the city. The seat in my van had become my couch, the van my home. Because solid sleep was out of the question, I sat and watched the daylight slowly consuming the night.

Five days seemed like an eternity.

Restless, about 8:30 A.M., I took a short drive around the campground and observed only a handful of fellow campers. My neighbors, however, enjoyed elements of comfort in luxurious campers. I wondered if any of them thought about the crazy guy in the van who endured cold and rain without the comforts of home. But I was feeling sorry for myself again.

I returned to campsite Twenty-Eight, which I now called "old 28," and took out my pen and notebooks. As I wrote in my journal, recording events of the previous day, I saw Buttons' head emerge from the sleeping bag, as if it were Groundhog's Day and she had come out to inspect the weather. I let her out of the van to go to the bathroom, and when she returned, she made a beeline for the sleeping bag.

I thought about author F. Scott Fitzgerald, the subject of the first book I had written, and about his October stay with his wife, Zelda, in 1921, at White Bear Lake, Minnesota. The big summer houses had closed for the season, with their wealthy occupants fleeing to St. Paul, but the Fitzgeralds decided to continue living in the home they had rented through the winter. During a drunken party, lack of attention to the central heating system resulted in frozen water pipes—the "Symbols of the Jazz Age" were sent packing.

Since the Fitzgeralds had been the sole residents to stay on that October, they must have watched the lights growing fewer night after night, and with them, they shared a sense of solitude. Theirs was a self-imposed isolation, and always with the realization that others would be coming to visit them. Still, I wondered how they had felt as they looked out over the lake at the last, dying flicker of light and, thereafter, darkness.

There are many kinds of seclusion, not all necessarily unpleasant. Like the Fitzgeralds, I watched the lights of the campground going out each night, all the time aware within a couple of days I would be alone. As at White Bear Lake with its mansions, these hardy campers, their own type of mansions on wheels, would be hastening back to the city and the corporate struggle. I think I looked forward to being alone at the campground, but I was lonely within my aloneness.

It was still raining at 10:00 A.M. when a ranger drove up and stopped at "old 28" to inform me they would be shutting off the water for the remainder of the season at 8:30 the next morning. Again I thought of Fitzgerald and the frozen water pipes while confronting my own situation. This would require me to get tougher and brace myself for what was to come.

According to the ranger, the other campers would leave as soon as running water, and flush toilets were no longer available. I told him I would stay on and make other arrangements, although I had no idea what those arrangements might be.

The loss of water was a tremendous obstacle, which I would have to overcome. I had not considered losing my drinking supply, but now this scenario was one to be reckoned with. Of course, I would stay on, water or no water, but I would have to make some drastic changes in my everyday activities.

I made a mental note to get to the bathrooms early next morning for what would be a final shower at Willow River. For a moment, I had considered pulling out, but with nowhere to go, staying on was an easy decision. Let them turn the water off at 8:30 A.M.; I would get in and out of the shower, albeit an eleventh hour ritual. After that—well, I did not care to think about "after."

I asked the ranger about the town of Burkhardt above Willow River Falls, and he gave me a short history of the quaint, little town. More important, he told me a few provisions could be purchased there, thus eliminating some of the longer drives into Hudson. I recalled driving through Burkhardt years before on a Sunday drive with my family along winding country roads and thought I remembered an old mill there.

I thanked the ranger for the information (they were always very courteous here) and drove out of the park and followed the quiet meandering road into Burkhardt. It was easy to pick out the site of the mill and the inn, which was once the home of the town's founder, Christian Burkhardt. The blue Burkhardt house, rich in history and architecture, was worth the five-minute drive in itself.

According to the ranger, Burkhardt, a German immigrant, had come to the Willow River area in 1868 because of poor health, after a stay in Buffalo, New York, where he had operated some flour mills. Arriving at Willow River, he purchased 600 acres of land along the stream and eventually increased his holdings to 1,000 acres.

Through construction of mills, which provided a sorely needed service to the farming community, he became inter-

ested in electrical power and returned to Germany to study a power plant on the Neckar River. When he returned to Willow River in 1891, he supervised construction of a power plant about a mile from the mill. Through his pioneering efforts, he was able to provide electrical power to the surrounding area.

In 1893, Burkhardt and the Andrews Electrical Company gave the town of Hudson its first electric lights. One of the first homes in Hudson to receive electric lighting was the Octagon House, now placed on the National Register of Historic Places and serving as St. Croix County's museum. I had visited the Octagon House some years before but remembered little about the interior.

Burkhardt called the community surrounding his mills, much of which is now within park boundaries, Willow River Falls but the name was short-lived. In 1880, Guy Daily, a member of the Wisconsin Assembly, pushed through legislation that changed the name of the community to Burkhardt in tribute to its founder.

As I stood on the riverbank overlooking the mill site, I longed to know more about the history of my "new home," and since I had nothing but time on my hands, I decided to take an in-depth look. Besides, by keeping busy and doing something useful, I would be helping myself keep things together mentally. The ranger had given me the name of Lorraine Jacobs, a local history buff, and I arranged a meeting with her.

Lorraine told me the Chippewa Indians, as well as some Dakota or Sioux paddled their way down the Willow River to the St. Croix, and it served as one of the main arteries for travel. With respect to the perilous waterfalls, the Indians knew where to portage, and I wondered about all the hard work that went into their canoe trips.

Lorraine also gave me the names of some other local historians and where I might pick up some brochures detailing Willow River history. It was already well beyond lunchtime, so I planned another odyssey into Hudson for what would really be an early supper.

I enjoyed a relaxing meal in Hudson, picked up more provisions, and took a short drive along the St. Croix. I tried not to think about all the times I had taken this same drive with my family over the years, but I could not ditch those feelings I tried to forget. I was able to cope with any hardships at Willow River, but the one struggle I could not reckon with, was the curse of memory.

Returning to the semi-deserted campground, Buttons and I took a brief walk as darkness descended. There were still a couple other campers staying for another night, and I knew the closing of running water in the morning would drive them from the park. I tried not to think about it.

Willow River is geographically a paradise—all the wonderful discomforts of the semi-wilderness with the real comforts of the city less than an hour away. I think my knowing that the city was easily accessible during any crisis made my stay much easier to cope with.

As I walked to the pay phones in the center of the campground to call those persons Lorraine Jacobs had mentioned, I knew I was in for a very cold night. The wind off the lake whipped ruthlessly through the forested lanes of the camping area and I tightened my collar in an attempt to stay warm. I have always been prone to attacks of bronchitis and pneumonia, and I needed neither at Willow River.

As Buttons and I walked back to the van, I noticed a camper whom we had seen on the way to the telephones had suddenly, in the span of a few moments, abandoned his campsite. I wondered if the inhabitant or inhabitants had merely left for supplies or had moved out permanently. At that particular moment, I believe I wanted them all to leave, each and every one of them. I wanted to be alone, and if and when the snow came, I would somehow adjust and stay on.

I fell asleep earlier than usual, lost in dreams of my childhood and a Minnesota winter.

6 Tuesday

I spent an extremely cold night. It was so cold, in fact, Buttons refused to get out of the van to go to the bathroom, even though she was wearing her sweater. Leaving Buttons in the van, I walked down to the bathrooms very early and took my last shower. I was in and out of the shower about an hour when park officials came by and shut down the water. Buttons and I took a quick walk around the campground and took inventory.

I had been given the name of local historian, Ben McDermott, and we had a ten o'clock appointment at his home to discuss Willow River history. Following a short drive from the park, we arrived at Ben's, and immediately began discussing logging on the Willow. The first dam, according to Ben, was built at the mouth of the Willow River, in what is today North Hudson, in 1847 or 1848 by James Parrington. Although Parrington died in 1849, the dam was completed a year later. Wisconsin had just become a state in 1848 with a population of 210,546.

Parrington's Mill, mistakenly called Pennington Mill, was destroyed by fire in 1862. But the Pennington Mill was not the only mill on the Willow at the time. John Bouran had erected a dam and sawmill in 1851 in the town of Bouchea where today the bridge over the Willow crosses Highway A at the foot of a hill. Bouran, said McDermott, provided living quarters for his workers by constructing a boarding house.

During the Civil War, Caleb Green and Charles Cox constructed a third mill on the Willow just east of today's bridge on Trout Brook Road. The Paradise Mill as it was called, became the first flourmill on the river, since its two predecessors had been sawmills. Known locally as Green's Mill, it made "Bird of Paradise" Flour. By 1870, Wisconsin boasted over a million people with mining, logging, and farming serving as the major industries. The Paradise was destroyed by a flood in 1894.

Christian Burkhardt built a flourmill on the Willow in 1868 behind today's co-op. A new mill he constructed about 1887 burned to the ground in 1975. Burkhardt, however, built a timber dam in 1892 at the site of Little Falls Dam in the present-day park. He and a partner rigged a transmission line into Hudson in 1893 and provided the community with its first electrical power. In both 1916 and 1934, the embankment was washed out, but the mills were rebuilt.

In 1897, Burkhardt and partner, James Andrews, purchased the flourmill at the mouth of the river and immediately discontinued the flour operation and converted it to electricity. That same year, Burkhardt bought out Andrews' interest in the mill.

Burkhardt constructed Willow Falls Dam in 1914 and then went home to Germany to order the generating equipment and waterwheels. World War I broke out while Burkhardt was in Germany. As a result, only one set of turbine and generator was shipped instead of the two he had ordered. He was able to buy a similar one, however, from Allis-Chalmbers in Milwaukee. During the mid-1920s, the other machine arrived from Germany. Another dam, the Mounds Dam, was constructed in 1925.

Ben McDermott knew his mills. In February 1942, he had begun working in a steam plant in Hudson, but on May 1, he transferred to Willow Falls Dam as operator. By summer, he operated three dams on the Willow—Little Falls Dam, Willow Falls (called High Dam), and Mounds Dam. Each day he could be seen at work at the two control wheels on the floor of the powerhouse.

Ben said he left the mills and went back to farming in November 1942, although he worked as a substitute operator for a few months. In February 1943, he went back to work in the steam plant. No one knew the Willow River area better than Ben McDermott. Before I left, Ben informed me that Robert McDiar, who had come with the Scotts from New Brunswick in mid-September 1850, discovered Willow Falls while working at the Pennington Mill.

Leaving McDermott, I rode over to the University of Wisconsin River Falls Campus, but the person I wanted to see was not in. I stopped in Hudson and chatted briefly with Willis Miller at the *Hudson Star-Observer*. Mr. Miller knew his local history, and I told him I would be back for a more in-depth discussion. I also talked with a woman at the historic Octagon House and visited the Valley Bookstore. Before returning to "old #28," we walked in Hudson's Prospect Park.

Like the night before, it was a very cold night. I sat up late into the night, watching an occasional automobile drive through the campground. As each approached, I was elated. Certainly, it would be my wife. She would not leave me here like this. She would jump out into my arms, all would be forgotten, and we'd go home together. That smile, the one that had been absent for quite some time, would light up her eyes and things would again be as they used to be. But as each of the cars continued past, I knew my fate had been sealed. Every cold night, I played the car ritual, and with each passing, my fledgling hopes were dashed.

7 Wednesday

I was up early and drove into Minneapolis and picked up my Dalmatian, Cassie. Both dogs accompanied me on a morning hike along the Willow Falls Trail. We sat and rested—or at least, I did—at the Scott homestead and took in the magnificent view of the valley. After a visit to the Little Falls Dam, we drove out of the park and crossed the St. Croix to the Minnesota side. At beautiful Afton State Park, the dogs and I hiked along the beach, Buttons taking ten steps to every one of Cassie's. Still, she never complained.

At one point, we discovered a stairway leading up a bluff from the water and climbed it for a view of the majestic St. Croix. Back at the beach, I climbed a deserted life guard tower. Sitting there, I was reminded of other times when my wife and I, hand-in-hand, had walked this very same beach. I remembered her hair blowing in the wind, that perfect smile, and, of course, that indefinable sparkle in her eyes. I climbed down from the tower and turned my back on the St. Croix.

In the tiny river town of Afton, I took a tour of the historic Afton House and looked at the bedrooms upstairs. My wife and I had always planned to stay at the Afton one day. Now I was here for a quick tour with two dogs out in the van. I wanted to visit the Afton Historical Society as well but was told it was closed. Before leaving the hamlet of Afton, I climbed a hill above the river and wandered into a cemetery to visit the grave of the wife of war correspondent, Ernie Pyle. I had always been interested in Ernie Pyle and his distinguished career. I was elated in finding Mrs. Pyle's grave here in Afton and was moved knowing that Ernie had long ago climbed this very same hill and stood where I was standing.

I went to bed fairly early. It was bitterly cold, and I was up several times during the night turning on the heat and looking for that ever-evasive car riding through the campground, that phantom that refused to serve as transfusion.

8 Thursday

Another quick drive into Minneapolis. There was no school that day, and I was elated when my seven-year-old daughter, Sarah, accompanied John, the dogs, and me back to Willow River. We walked the Willow Falls Trail, and I told Sarah repeatedly how much I missed her and everyone else. Even her mother.

Back at the campsite, the kids fished in the lake with John catching a crappie. It was so nice having two of my children with me again. I wished my other two daughters—Stacy and Stephanie—had been along, and, of course, their mother. John and Sarah also fished at Little Falls Dam but with no luck. It was I who had the luck—just having them with me.

We hiked along the Trout Brook Trail, which followed the trout stream. The dogs ran far ahead, but this trail was very level with few surprises and much easier to walk than the others. We met a woman on the trail who told us about a third falls in the park. She informed us we had to leave the park, drive through the town of Burkhardt and, eventually, we'd come to another, albeit smaller section, of the park.

Driving through Burkhardt, I looked at the inn and wished I had the money to buy such a place and convert it into a bed and breakfast. Beyond the town, we spotted the park sign and drove onto a dirt road looking for the falls. Sarah and I hiked a trail while John tried his luck with a fishing pole. Meeting a fisherman on the short trail, he directed us to the falls, which were right around the corner on the winding path.

The Upper Falls were magnificent, but climbing down to the Lower Falls was even more breathtaking. After we crossed a little bridge, the falls roared above us, only partially concealing the giant tree roots, which protruded from the rugged cliffs. All our faces were wet from spray, and, as we stood there admiring the falls, I felt as if I was a character in a science fiction movie I had seen as a kid. The falls simply did not look real. They were so large, so powerful, and descended upon us from different angles.

John pulled in what looked like four baby trout. He threw the fish back in, of course, and ran along the bank watching them swim away. My eyes followed him, then switched to Sarah, and then the dogs. It was almost like old times, and I prayed the time would go slowly.

The kids roared with laughter when I lost my balance on a slippery rock and plunged on my behind into the river. The water was not deep, but deep enough to completely give me a soaking. I think I needed that laugh. I had had so few. And I think the kids needed it even more than I did. Funny, but I had never realized that falling into a river could be so much fun.

Before I took the kids home, we saw a shooting star jolt across the evening sky.

9 Friday

It had been a very cold night. I was surprised, upon waking, to see three hardy souls camping in a tent just across the way. They had not been there when Buttons and I had gone to sleep, and they had been very quiet in setting up their canvas home.

Taking a short walk, Buttons and I came upon three startled deer that stood in the path as if they were statues. This would not do, of course, and ferocious little Buttons, all nine-and-one-half pounds of her, charged them. The deer leaped into the thicket as Buttons looked at me for approval.

We drove down to Little Falls Dam and then left the park and stopped at Mounds Dam. I thought of many things that Ben McDermott had told me about the mills. Heading toward Hudson, I saw two more deer in a field. In town, I paid another visit to the Valley Bookstore and walked out a little poorer.

Driving over to the Minnesota side of the river, we started to walk along the trail to the beach. The wind was so bitterly cold that we turned back, retreating toward where the van was parked. We did hike to an overlook for a splendid view of the valley. I strained to see beyond Hudson and guessed approximately where our site at Willow River was. But it was difficult to keep from looking back over my shoulder in the direction of Minneapolis, my wife, and my children.

I took a historic walking tour in the town of Afton, visiting antique shops, the waterfront, and the Afton House. Before leaving Afton, I again drove to the hilltop and paused at the grave of Mrs. Pyle.

Back at Willow River, Buttons snuggled into my sleeping bag early, and I soon followed her. We spent the coldest night of our stay so far and my thoughts of my family kept me awake long into the night.

10 Saturday

After surviving a very cold night, Buttons and I drove into Minneapolis and picked up John and Cassie. We drove slowly through the park looking for deer—John counted them and kept daily records—but we did not see any. I had found that the best time for seeing deer was about five o'clock in the evening until dark.

As John and I walked through the campground, we decided to try and hike all the trails in the park in one day. John was more optimistic than I was and a much better hiker. We took a short trek on the Lake Trail and met only two fellow-hikers, both women. There were many deer droppings along the lake so the animal population had been out in force. It was very cold along the lake, and we were only too glad to find our way back to the campsite.

Next came the Little Falls Trail and this, undoubtedly, was the toughest trail in the park. The trail took us through deep woods and ravines and the high, roller coaster hills took their toll on our endurance. The multi-colored trees were gorgeous, however, and we paused at several vistas to take in the prairie and the panorama of the St. Croix. I found myself unconsciously staring at the St. Croix because deep within I knew my family lived beyond its sacred shores.

Entering the White Tail Trail, we again reveled at scenic overlooks, and although the trail was known for its abundance of deer, we saw none. We took a smaller, more intimidating spur off the White Tail and followed a long-closed, narrow, blacktop highway. Weeds grew prominently from cracks in the highway, and as we passed a farm, we saw a woman climbing aboard a tractor to begin a day's labor.

As I studied the weed-covered road, I thought of H.P. Lovecraft's poem, "The Ancient Track." I had first read the poem as a teenager and had envisioned the track to look very much like the road we were following. That poem was in the book, *Collected Poems by Lovecraft,* and that revelation reminded me that this particular poem was in the book, which still reposed in my library at home. And, of course, any thought of home was like a stab in the heart, and I was soon feeling sorry for myself.

My pain faded somewhat as we turned onto the Knapweed Trail and followed it across the prairie and through a beautiful grove of trees. I sat down and rested on the pine-needled path in the midst of a pine forest, as it seemed like a perfect place to rest. The wind could not reach us here, but we had to be careful to avoid the poison ivy patch that beckoned just behind us.

We followed three circular trails, which branched out from the Knapweed. John insisted on seeing what lay beyond every trail, so I, too, was hooked into a Lewis and Clark type of exploration. After emerging from a small grove of pines, we made our way back to the campsite for something to eat, abandoning any thoughts of hiking other trails within and without the park's borders.

In the evening, we drove into Burkhardt and went into the Willow River Inn to watch the Minnesota Twins in the Major League Baseball playoffs. Although the Twins lost seven to six on Pat Sheridan's eighth inning homerun, the Twins still led the series two to one. I could not help noticing a picture of a bird on a sign in the bar as I sipped a bottle of beer that I nursed through nine innings of baseball. The sign read: "I'd rather eat worms than drive a Chevy."

Back at the campground, John, the dogs, and I climbed down the stairs to the lake, talking all the while about things we had done together. I pulled three wood ticks off Buttons as John fished for a few quiet moments.

Leaving the park once more, we drove along a dirt road and found an old, abandoned, rusty, steel bridge over the river. John fished from the bridge while I walked with the dogs along the bank of the river. Both of us watched as two men in a boat came downriver and had a tight squeeze passing under the bridge. One of the men yelled to us that he hoped the old bridge wouldn't collapse while they were beneath it. One of the anglers told us that northern, bass, and sunfish could all be caught along this stretch of the river. Watching John, who was having one bite after another, I wasn't surprised.

Back in the park, we began hiking the White Deer Trail, and along the way, encountered six deer and a red fox.

We followed a doe into the woods and it kept stopping, as if frozen, with a perpetual staring fixation. Soon, the doe disappeared, and we made our way back to the van.

It was becoming an incredibly cold evening as John fished at the Mound Pond Dam. In two hours, he hauled in eight trout and two bass, all of which had to be set free. I don't know what possible connection there could have been, but as I sat there watching him, I remembered myself as a young boy. I had in those days of the late 1940s, a pet chicken named "Voo,"—"Hincky," "Dinky," and "Parley" had all passed on. Voo was so tame he sat on my shoulder and responded like a dog when his name was called. Soon we had to leave him with a relative at a farm, and the farmer promised me he would take care of him. Take care of him he did: After visiting the farmer a month later and enjoying a delicious dinner, the farmer asked, "Did you enjoy the chicken, Jackie?" I answered, "Yes, sir." The farmer laughed, bellowing, "You should have! You just ate your pet chicken!" I remember screaming and running out of that house. I never ate chicken again. But John was catching fish, not chickens, and when he yelled, "Dad, look at this one I caught," I turned and forgot about the haunting chicken episode.

We retired late that night, the van protecting us from the cold wind but not the night chill. I looked at John while he was sleeping. I hoped the weekend would never end.

11 Sunday

We spent a bitterly cold night, but by mid-morning, the sun was shining and the temperature had reached a tropical thirty-eight degrees. Sitting at my little picnic table while John fished, my mind drifted back many years to when I had met my wife. I was playing piano in a little combo when she walked in to the dance. Initially, she did not care for me, and it took awhile before she became interested. I was certain she did not care for me now either. As I sat there in the woods watching the leaves blow lifelessly across the table, I wondered if she ever did care for me.

The wind picked up in the afternoon, but when the temperature soared to fifty degrees, I was enjoying a real heat wave. As I stooped to pick a wood tick off Cassie, a woodchuck wobbled slowly into the campsite. He regarded us with curiosity but was in no hurry whatsoever to get anywhere.

Again I was haunted by that 1967 interruption in my life that had once before taken me from my family. When I returned home a year-and-a-half later, it was to a new home. My father had passed away and most of the treasures I had owned as a child—baseball cards, comic books, Big Little Books, and pulp magazines—were no longer mine. It was a sad, different situation but with the same insecurity and uncertainty that plagued me now. And, of course, back then as well as now, I was totally unprepared for it.

In mid-afternoon, we drove into Burkhardt and stopped at the co-op to buy John some night crawlers at $1.50 per dozen. Returning to the campsite, John scurried down the stairs to the lake and was rewarded with six fat perch. It was time to go hiking.

While exploring the Hidden Ponds Nature Trail, we were greeted by a family of chipmunks. We visited three ponds along the trail, encountering ducks, snakes, and squirrels. Buttons and Cassie were especially interested in the latter.

Leaning against a stately oak, I thought I discovered some evidence of oak wilt on the valuable tree that served as my staff. When the oak wilt fungus attacks and disrupts the flow of sap, few, if any, of the trees recover. The fungus, especially in red and black oaks, often enters these trees through root grafts and open wounds.

Leaving the trail, I sat at the amphitheater while John again fished. My memories always seemed to catch up with me at times like this, and this particular rest period was no exception. I was back in Minneapolis twenty-two years before, about to go away. My mother, father, and Dodo accompanied me to the railroad station and watched me board the train with tears in their eyes. As the train pulled out in the night, I watched the lights of small towns that dotted the Midwest prairies like well-lit ornaments on some gigantic Christmas tree. I missed my Minnesota then, I recalled, although I had only left her hours before. I pledged to never leave her again, but now, I had broken that promise. Would I be forever breaking promises, and, more important, hearts?

Upon walking into the new house, after one and one-half years, I couldn't wait to see my faithful springer spaniel, Rex. Instead, I was crushed upon walking into my new realm. Poor Rex, now old and senile, no longer remembered me. It seemed like the end of the world, for I had dreamed of this reunion with my dog many times over that dreadful year behind bars. But then came salvation. I went to my piano and began playing; the first time I had touched a keyboard in nearly two years. As I began fumbling on the keys, I sang one of the old songs my family and I had always enjoyed together. Rex jumped up, tail wagging in the air, and began licking my face frantically. He remembered me. It took my voice and the piano to jar his memory. Good old Rex! I was so happy I cried.

I realized I was crying then at the amphitheater at Willow River, too. Like Rex, my old home, my childhood possessions, my wife, family, new home, and everything I ever loved had vanished in a heartbeat. And there was no hope of retrieving any of it.

Two fishermen in a boat crying out simultaneously as each pulled in a crappie rescued me from my memories. At that same moment, my son walked back from his angler's tour of the shoreline. We returned to the campsite just as a squirrel shimmied up one of the trees on our "property."

John scampered down the stairs to resume fishing and the bitter loneliness came rushing back upon me. It was getting late in the afternoon, and soon I would be alone again with only Buttons for companionship. I think at that moment, I almost loathed the school system for keeping my son away from me for five days out of every week. Sundays were indeed tough because they marked the beginning of another week of loneliness. For a week I would be trapped within my own thoughts, and I had never been an optimistic sort of person to begin with. I was never able to picture the future because I was always lost in the past. It was a dangerous condition for someone in my neurotic position.

John caught nineteen perch before losing his line on a tree branch. He was upset because he had set his goal at twenty. All the fish were released and anxiously swam away to rejoin the others. We left the park and went into Hudson for supper but soon returned looking for deer on the gentle hills and in the sloping valleys. Walking along one of the prairie trails, John counted twenty-five deer in an hour and a half.

As night descended, we parked our van on a hill by the ranger station and followed the White Tail Trail into the woods. It was cold and very dark and easy to imagine all kinds of things lurking in the blackness around each bend. Our flashlight beam cast an eerie glow, and occasionally we could see the clear night sky with its many stars. One star stood out in particular, and why, I don't know, but it made me feel closer to my wife. The orb soon became our only source of light as the flashlight battery died, and we were plunged into blackness. If there were deer along the trail, we could not have seen them, even if they stood upon our toes.

Returning to the van, much in the method of the way I played blind man's buff as a kid, we started out for Minneapolis. I did not want to take John and Cassie home, but I knew I must. We stopped briefly in North Hudson and walked out on the old dam where the Willow River emptied into the St. Croix. Despite the lateness of the hour, there was a man fishing from a ledge below the dam. It was a very dangerous thing to do, and as we walked back to the van, we hoped the man would not fall into the roaring river.

Leaving John and Cassie in Minneapolis, Buttons and I returned to the campground about midnight. As I rearranged some things in the back of the van, a red fox walked right out in front of me and studied me in my glass prison. After he departed, I took a short stroll through the campground. There were no lights now, no voices. The only sounds I heard came from the woods, and, as I circled the eerie campground, it became apparent that we were the only campers spending the night in the frigid campground.

It was very cold when I finally went to bed. Buttons, wearing her wool sweater, climbed into my sleeping bag, and I saw her no more until that tiny, furry head emerged the next morning.

12 Monday

I woke up to cold morning air. Following a makeshift breakfast, I drove into Hudson and visited the newspaper office to set up an interview with Willis Miller. After agreeing on a meeting for Wednesday, anytime after 9:00 A.M., I telephoned Edna Gwin and set up an appointment for 10:00 A.M. Tuesday.

I took a stroll down to Lakefront Park in town and perused the boats anchored in the harbor. There were many geese exploring the park, and the crunching of leaves under my feet assured me that winter was not far off. It was a pleasant walk, however, as I tried to figure out if I was following the geese or if they were following me.

Taking in the Nutrena Mill across the street, I was reminded of August Derleth's story, "The Lonesome Place." The author, while growing up in Sauk City, Wisconsin, had always been afraid of the mill when passing by it in the evening. There was nothing to be afraid of here at Willow River, however, but Derleth's eerie conception of the mill made me acutely aware of my loneliness. I smiled while observing a sign on the Nutrena Mill in front of me which read, "Duck Crossing."

Continuing my walk along the St. Croix, which paralleled downtown Hudson, with a host of ducks, geese, and pigeons, I came to an abandoned building bearing a huge padlock. Nearby was a deserted playground that I knew in summer must be a noisy center of activity. Now only the wind blew and the leaves crackled beneath my feet. It was a lonely time of year, and I fought my depression by playing with Buttons. Walking out on a rickety old fishing dock near three huge rocks, I sat down and gave in to my memories. I was truly my own worst enemy.

In the afternoon, I hiked in figure-eight fashion around the campground. I read some passages from a volume of Nathaniel Hawthorne, followed by a late afternoon nap. I think it must have been the cold that woke me up after darkness fell. I was ill and burning up with fever. I remembered I had included a thermometer in my travel bag and quickly took it out. My temperature was 102. There was no need to eat supper; I only wanted to sleep.

13 Tuesday

Feeling very sick, I slept on and off throughout the day. I did not eat throughout this period as I fought the influenza by resting. I simply did not have the energy to get up and make myself eat something. Coupled with the flu attack was my old nemesis—neuritis neuralgia—a painful facial condition, which had plagued me since childhood and runs in the family. I lay there thinking of past illnesses. Foremost was the memory of my being bed-ridden with pneumonia shortly after getting married. My wife had placed a thermometer in my mouth, and as I lay there sucking on it, she came rushing back into the room screaming, "Oh, my God, I gave you the rectal thermometer by mistake." It was not a pleasant moment, but just then, I would have given everything I owned (which wasn't much) to go back and relive that albeit gross situation.

I was too sick to enjoy what was to be the warmest day of my Willow River stay. The temperature reached seventy degrees, but I was too ill to leave the van and bask in the sun. I did manage to telephone Edna Gwin regarding Willow River history and interviewed her briefly. Like the others, she was a storehouse of information, and her pleasant voice was perhaps the only respite from illness and depression I had all day.

14 Wednesday

Slept all day. Too sick to do anything! For the second consecutive day I ate nothing.

Since I remembered my appointment with Willis Miller that morning, I did, however, gather my strength for the ride into Hudson. As busy as I knew Mr. Miller was that day and every day, I found him to be a most cordial human being. He gave me several brochures detailing Hudson and Willow River history, and I purchased a couple chapbooks he felt would be helpful in my investigation. We spent nearly an hour together, and he related that I was welcome to stop back at any time.

Of course I never revealed anything pertaining to my marital breakup, and our conversations dealt mainly with historical aspects of the region. He seemed to me a throwback to an earlier era when professional men, regardless of their schedule, always took a few minutes out of each day to talk to fellow human beings. I liked him and wished there were more like him.

This quick drive in and out of Hudson constituted my only exercise of the day. It rained in the evening as I tried in vain to sit up and read some Hawthorne. I let Buttons out to do her business but watched her frolic through the campground from the van. My main concern was that I would be too sick on the weekend to allow John to come for his next visit. I could tolerate the illness, perhaps, but I could not endure another separation from my son.

15 Thursday

He was here again last night! He disturbs my dreams most nights and last night was no exception. And like all those other nights over the past decade, I woke up screaming, and, despite the chill, damp with perspiration. My nocturnal yell awakened Buttons, and I was glad there was no one else in the campground.

He, this dark, grotesque figure, had been affecting my sleep for twenty years now. When I was working on a very real prison road gang in the South—if southern Missouri qualifies as South—during the mid-1960s, waiting to be transferred to Leavenworth, he was on that same work crew. I had never talked to him; no one had. He was only seventeen years old, but he was serving twenty years for rape. In prison you talk with, eat with, and play sports with every kind of murderer, robber, and criminal imaginable, but you draw the line when it comes to rapists and child molesters. You don't care what your neighbors are in for with the exception of sex offenders. It takes a little bit of getting used to. At first you do care who your associates are: you are afraid, and, of course, sorry for yourself. But after a few weeks, you are so demoralized by the system, you no longer care if you ever get out or what happens to you.

I don't know why he approached *me* of all people that morning as we were preparing to go out on the road detail. He stopped in front of me and whispered, "I can't stand it any longer; I'm going to make a run for it." Although I never wanted to talk with him, I answered, "Don't do it, man; they'll blow your [bleeping] head off." With that he walked away, and we joined a handful of prisoners and two guards with shotguns to march out the gate.

We had been working for about fifteen to twenty minutes picking up large rocks and throwing them into a dump truck. Of course at the end of the day, that very same truck would drive back over the course of the road and dump these rocks back onto the roadbed. The following morning, we would be out with the very same shotgun guards picking up the very same large rocks. Our government is shrewd that way, and who would want to look for new rocks anyway!

On this particular morning, when one of the guards seemed to be distracted, I saw the young man break for a gully and the woods beyond. Guards are ordered to fire two warning shots, then shoot at the legs. There was no warning and no aiming below the belt. One of the guards fired and blew off the back of the boy's head right in front of me. I cried like a baby for I had never seen anyone killed before and certainly not like this. Could I have prevented this awful act? Perhaps I should have hit him, stopped him somehow, but I never believed he had meant what he proposed to do. Prisoners talked about escaping every day, but no one ever did. Still, I had often wondered if I could have prevented this terrible tragedy.

For twenty years, the nightmare was always the same. This headless dead boy would walk towards me holding his head under his arm. He would stand there and then whisper, "I'm going to make a break for it." I was never sure if the voice was coming from the head under his arm or the severed bloody flesh upon his neck. The dream would never go beyond that point, and I would wake myself by screaming.

I didn't really need that dream this morning. As Buttons and I stepped from the van, I tried desperately to get my mind off the dream. But where else could I turn but to the reality of my estranged situation. One was as bad as the other, and I shivered either from the cold or from the shock of the two very real nightmares.

Before making myself a bowl of cold cereal, I made one for Buttons. Adding a little somewhat-hardened peanut butter to a couple pieces of bread, we breakfasted. I was feeling slightly better from my illness of three days, and I did not have a temperature. But I needed rest even though I was afraid to go back asleep and be confronted with a repeat performance of the dream.

It was a good day for sleeping, however. Heavy clouds were in the sky, and the rains came immediately upon completion of our meal. They continued throughout the day as I napped through the morning, attempting to get back on track from both my illness and my memories.

Skipping lunch, I took Buttons for a short walk in the rain that afternoon. It was not a good decision on my part as both of us were drenched by the time we returned to the van. A couple hours later, my clothing still damp, we went back out for a second hike in the rain. Although I was sick and feeling weak, I felt I had to get out of the van and walk somewhere, anywhere.

On the trail we met a man with a large dog. I quickly picked up Buttons as the larger animal jumped all over me, its muddy front paws mashing mud into my clothes. There was no apology from the man or the animal, and we continued on our way despite the rain and the mud. The fog was steadily moving in from across the Willow so we turned into the mist and made our way back to the ghostly camp.

In late afternoon, we finished off most of our remaining food. With the swirling fog and penetrating rain, we sat in the van, I reading a little more Hawthorne, Buttons curled up in her favorite corner. About five-thirty we rode down to the beach, seeing four deer along the way. It was still raining but not nearly as heavily as it had been all day.

The beach was deserted. I left Buttons in the car so her fur could dry. The fog was London-soup now as I hiked along the waterfront towards Little Falls Dam. I paused at the beach shelter to get out of the rain, and as I did so, I glimpsed a man walking up from the water in the semi-darkness. His appearance seemed strikingly weird, or perhaps I thought so from reading too much Nathaniel Hawthorne and M.R. James. Strange, however, that I had not seen him go down to the water before this. It was almost as if he walked out of the river itself.

As the stranger disappeared into the fog, my eyes beheld a light upon the bluff across the lake. The light was emanating from a castle-like structure high atop the bluffs, and like the man "who walked out of the water," its eerie glow taunted my imagination. Further down the bluff, I saw another light, fainter than the other, but one of the few beacons peeping out of the intense fog and rain.

Walking back to the van, I saw a truck that had evidently been parked next to it, pulling away into the darkness. The mystery of the water-walking man was solved. I was dismayed to discover that the stranger had deposited a pile of garbage on the parking lot, and before getting into my own vehicle, I picked up the intruder's debris. I am not a happy camper when humans threaten nature with their spiteful collections of refuse. Below the dam were colonies of ferns, mosses, liverworts, jewelweeds, and other species that thrive on the damp, cool ravines and cliff faces. The trees, shrubs, ferns, and wildflowers are threatened daily from such carelessness.

I glimpsed five more deer feeding on the hillside on my way back to camp. Buttons and I sat in the van until about ten-thirty that evening when we departed for another short stroll through the deserted campground. The rain, however, was coming down more than ever, and the fog had thickened so that it was difficult to see where we were going. Returning to the van, I began arranging the bedrolls when I saw the glow of headlights piercing the fog on the road. Again my heart pounded. Could it be her coming at last to get me and say everything was all right?

My heart sank as a very classy Cadillac passed by, reminding me of St. Paul gangsters and Chicago's Al Capone. Yes, I do have an imagination, and many had been the time when I had passed by such gangster sanctuaries in St. Paul as Hollyhocks and the Green Lantern. Strange, I fancied, that such a luxurious automobile should pass through a deserted campground during the night for its occupants did not appear to be the roughing-it type.

I went to sleep with thoughts of my wife. I wondered what she was doing and if she ever thought about where I might be and what I was doing. Of course she didn't care, how could I expect her to when our relationship was definitely over and done. Her face filled my dreams and the boy with no head did not reappear.

16 Friday

I slept little during the night, however. The fog had thickened beyond belief, and the rain drummed upon the roof of the van, igniting my imagination with flights of fancy. Despite the weather, I took Buttons for a walk at 3:45 A.M. Although the rain was steady, there was absolutely no thunder or lightning.

I did manage a few catnap sessions between four o'clock and seven o'clock. As I took Buttons for another walk in the rain, a noisy flock of geese flew over us. I could not help thinking that the geese had a place to go, and I wished with all my heart, I could trade Willow River for even five minutes with my estranged wife. But, of course, I had chosen my own destiny and, like that cell two decades before, I was on my own as a prisoner all over again.

Buttons and I descended the stairs that led down to the lake from "old 28." It was a precarious descent since the fog was still enveloping us, although it seemed to be moving slowly out over the lake. Although the fog seemed to be receding, the flu or cold or whatever was causing my up-and-down fever, was not. Despite my condition, I was excited because I would be leaving in an hour to again pickup John for the weekend.

Following the Friday ritualistic drive into Minneapolis to pick up my son and Cassie, we parked in Hudson and walked along the water front park. As we passed by numerous fishing crafts, we were joined by scores of geese and ducks that, like ourselves, did not mind the light rain. We bought a quick lunch while in Hudson, as well as a few provisions and returned to Willow River.

John pulled in sixteen perch from the lake beneath our campsite. He was pretty proud of himself and so was I. When the fish stopped biting, we walked along the Willow River Trail in the rain and increasing cold. Cassie became so covered with mud that I picked her up and threw her into the lake. John followed my actions by tossing Buttons in after her. We laughed heartily until the larger of the two animals bathed us by shaking water from her body.

On the way back, a woodchuck, not the least bit timid, walked up and sniffed me not once but four times. We stopped at the ranger station, and John turned in his stamped trail passport proving he had walked all major trails in the park. He was rewarded with a "Wise Explorer" badge and certificate. I talked with the lady ranger for some time about the Scott Homestead and the mills along the Willow. Like all personnel at Willow River, she was well informed, and I furthered my education as to local history and lore.

John and I rode up and down the park road for a steady two hours after leaving the station and counted forty-seven deer on both sides of the road. We also saw a stray cat walking along the road, and we wondered from whence it had come. I would have been only too glad to have taken it, but I feared that he or she would only serve as a meal for Cassie.

We drove to Hudson late that night. Driving along the highway that fronts Willow River State Park, we approached a railroad crossing and saw flashing red lights up ahead. A train had demolished a car where the road crossed the track, its occupant undoubtedly killed in the crash. Returning from Hudson, we saw the smashed car sitting alongside the road, and although I said nothing to John, my mind drifted back to Christmas 1960 when my own brother had been killed in an auto wreck.

My mind did not stop there. I also thought about two old friends Bob and Roger. In those long-ago college days, I was playing in a musical combo at a club in northeast Minneapolis to help pay my tuition. Always supportive, my two friends had come to the club, and Bob, especially, danced the night away. At the end of the evening, they offered me a ride home, but I told them I had my own car. As they left, I thanked them for coming. It was the last time I ever saw them. On the way home, their car collided with another, and both my friends were killed.

Why did life have to be so cruel? My brother, father, friends were now only memories as my marriage was becoming. I wondered why my wife and I could never communicate, and if we had, would things be any different now. Perhaps it was too late to specualate.

I stopped the van on the highway as a raccoon stepped slowly out in front of us. Driving into the park through the rain and light mist, my eyes were drawn to the light from the house atop the bluff. One lonely light, and like myself, in exile.

I was surprised that night to see the Cadillac return. Again it moved slowly through the campground, its occupant looking for someone or something I could not fathom. Never

did it come during the day but performed its mysterious ritual only at night.

About midnight, John woke up with a fever, and I drove him back to Minneapolis. I felt sorry for the little guy but also sorry for myself because I was being deprived of his company for perhaps another week. When I returned to Willow River early in the morning, I couldn't sleep. I sat in the darkness picturing skyscrapers crashing to the ground, the eyes of my wife smiling at me from across the miles. It was then that I realized, I would see that smile no more, and the skyscrapers had taken their last tumble.

17 Saturday

An early morning telephone call brought good news. John was feeling better, and he and Cassie were itching to come back to Willow River. I drove to Minneapolis, picked them up, and stopped in Hudson on the way back to "old 28." The public library in Hudson was holding a book sale, and never in my life during good times or bad could I stay away from such low-budget literary events. While John looked somewhat bored, I trudged out of the library with two heaping shopping bags full of books. I would certainly not run out of literature during my sojourn at Willow River.

The rest of the morning was spent walking around the campground at Willow River. A hasty lunch was gobbled down and the four of us—a man, a boy, and two dogs—headed back across the St. Croix River to the Minnesota side. We drove along the winding road that skirted the river and stopped at an antique store in the town of Afton. Walking up a hill that overlooked the valley, we walked through the little cemetery and paused once again at the grave of the wife of war correspondent/writer Ernie Pyle.

The early afternoon was spent hiking in Afton State Park. The view from the bluffs was magnificent, and when we followed the winding stairway into the valley, we crossed an old bridge and entered the woods. Eventually we were deposited on a beach along the St. Croix. Being October, there were no swimmers, of course, and we climbed the deserted lifeguard "tower" and peered across the river toward Willow River.

John had, of course, brought along his fishing pole, but after a frustrating hour for him, although relaxing respite for me, we lost ourselves in the woods amid the labyrinth of trails. Although John had caught no fish, he was in good spirits, and the dogs ran ahead of us as always, exploring every nook and cranny of the forest.

Leaving Afton State Park, we drove towards Prescott, Wisconsin, crossed the bridge and took a brief stroll through the Carpenter-St. Croix Nature Center. Back in the van, we rode back across the state line into Minnesota at Hastings and walked about the historic district. The river town is a walk back in time with its Greek Revival buildings and historic houses.

I found out later that the Dakota Indians called the area "O-wo-bopte," meaning "the place to dig tipsianna"—a certain desired turnip. In 1819 supply boats on their way to Fort Snelling were stopped here because of the river's low water level. Lieutenant W. G. Oliver led a detachment of troops to guard the provisions over the winter where they established a camp in a grove of trees. For the next thirty-four years, the area was called Oliver's Grove.

The natural river harbor and fertile farmland attracted settlers to the grove, and in 1853, the town's four original settlers dropped their names into a hat. When the name of Henry Hastings Sibley was drawn, the town was given its official name of Hastings.

Devouring an early supper in Hastings, we drove back to Willow River, parked the car along the side of the park drive, and hiked the Valley Park Trail. Although we found a few animal tracks, we saw little wildlife. In the evening, we drove into Burkhardt and stopped at the local saloon. Somehow the two of us made a coke and chips last nine innings of televised baseball as the Minnesota Twins captured game one of the World Series ten to one.

18 Sunday

We spent a cold night in the van, and John was still sleeping when I took Cassie and Buttons out for their early morning walk. I was glad the frequently recurring nightmare had left me alone that night for I would have frightened John to no end. Leaves and twigs crunched under my feet as my dogs and I strolled about the campground, all the while keeping an eye on the van in case John should awaken and wonder where we had gone.

I remembered a long-ago family vacation to Oregon when the kids were little and my wife and I were still close. Stacy and Stephanie teased little John from the time we left Minnesota until we entered Crater Lake National Park. I had warned the girls several times as we headed West that by torturing their little brother relentlessly, he might get so angry that he would fight back. My premonition was accurate. John found himself somewhere in the Cascades and taught the girls he was someone to be reckoned with. My wife and I laughed all the way home and the return trip was a relaxing, peaceful affair for all.

A 1975 trip to Mackinac Island in Michigan was recalled after that, and I smiled remembering Stacy, then age four, and Stephanie, a big two, getting into a fistfight in a crowded fudge shop on the island. I pulled them apart just as Stephanie went down from a crushing right to the jaw in full view of all the store's patrons. My wife and I were embarrassed and spankings were applied once we left the store and took refuge from the crowds that poured in and out of it.

We really were a closely-knit family in those golden days. We laughed together, and, like any family, cried together. Now I wondered if my wife ever cried thinking of me. She cried so easily over late-night movies but did she really care that our marriage had been broken up, or was I the only one? The kids cared so much. Their tears continued to flow like spring rain, and I must admit my own were not about to quit. Occasionally one of the kids would tell me that they saw their mother crying alone in her bedroom, and I wondered if she was crying because her pride was hurt or whether some of those tears were for me. If so, why had she never communicated with me or allowed me to discuss my own feelings? Then I would realize that it was I who lacked a means of communication, and I had nobody to blame but myself.

I carried with me much of the blame for our breakup through those pristine woods of Willow River. No matter how I looked at the situation, much of it was my fault. I wondered what my children were thinking when they looked at me, confused as to how their parents could separate, and somehow I wanted to run away all over again. Willow River, despite the cold, was a good experience for me. In this solitude I could put my thoughts together although there was truly no solution to the problem. My life had changed drastically, and from now on I would drift through life alone trying not to look back, knowing well that I must.

I made John breakfast, if cold cereal and peanut butter sandwiches can be considered a meal, and we started out along the Willow River Trail. Buttons and Cassie were elated to be together and I wondered how the little poodle could keep up with those bounding leaps of my mighty Dalmatian. Somehow she did, however, even though she must have taken ten or twenty steps to every one of Cassie's.

The dogs took off after a small black snake that had crossed our trail at the wrong time, at least from the snake's point of view. After an ear shattering outpouring of barking and kennel name-calling, thrashing through the tall grass, and stampeding back and forth before us, the search was called off. The snake had evidently escaped into some hole in the earth, undoubtedly a little bit better for wear.

We did very little the remainder of the day. The weather was cold, and, although there was very little rain, I found myself turning on the heater in the van to keep us warm. It was too cold to fish, and John contented himself with playing with the dogs and slipping off into occasional nap sessions. I knew he was not feeling as well as he put on, but I took delight in knowing he wanted to be with me despite feeling ill. In fact that night, he begged me to telephone his mother and ask her for permission to remain another day at Willow River. That would mean, however, his missing school that day and I talked him out of it.

We called his mother from the campground that afternoon to let her know John was having a good time. Of course, I did not talk to her. I deposited some coins, dialed her number, realizing that it was now "her" number and not "ours," and handed him the receiver. While they chatted, I wanted to rush to that same receiver myself and pour out my feelings. Whether it was pride, cowardice, shame, or sham, I wasn't certain, but as much as I wanted to, I could not.

I took John and Cassie home that night and watched their mother open the door to let them in. I watched her a moment to see if she would look at me, but she closed the door without doing so. I was not surprised nor could I blame her. Still, I don't think she had looked at me at all over the last year of our marriage. I could not identify the catalyst but somehow she had seemed to stop caring for me.

It was a lonely ride back to Willow River that evening. As I drove through St. Paul along the interstate, I could not help but look at the city lights that soon faded behind me like snuffed out candles. When I saw a farmhouse along the highway, I reasoned there were families within, sharing, loving, and doing all those things that families do so well together when there is harmony.

How long could I stay at Willow River? Where would I go upon leaving? I pondered those questions and finally fell asleep, only to be awakened in the middle of the night by my own screaming. Even that appalling nightmare from a tragedy that had taken place twenty years earlier would not let me sleep.

19 Monday

I was up with the sun and eager to go for a walk. The melancholy thoughts that had been plaguing me during the night still had me in their grip, and I told myself I might be able to run away from them if I could walk briskly through the nearby fields. According to a brochure I had picked up at the Visitor Center, Wisconsin had presently only about 13,000 acres of original prairie lands. This was a disheartening statistic to say the least, since in 1830, there were about 7,500,000 acres of prairie/savanna. Willow River State Park is situated on the northern-most edge of the tall-grass and was once known as the "Hudson Prairie."

Walking out on the prairie trails while reading a brochure, I looked for the thick, white flower heads of wild quinine that supposedly grew along the road and paths. Wild quinine had saved many pioneers on the prairies and certainly many soldiers in the Pacific. I recalled actor Robert Taylor stretched out on a cot, clothes drenched in perspiration, while fighting both malaria and the enemy in a World War II movie whose title I could not recall. At the turn of the century, quinine was the only known drug to have had any appreciable effect on malaria. During the period between the two world wars, extensive research revealed that several synthetic compounds were more effective.

Like our American wild quinine, I recalled reading some time ago, the cinchona flowers, native to the Andes of South America, are small and most often creamy-white or rose in color. Four species of cinchona were cultivated in Java, India, and Sri Lanka, and the quinine was extracted from the bark of trees.

Many of the native prairie grasses in Wisconsin survived because the Willow River area is a dry prairie. The brochure stated that many introduced, non-native plants cannot compete with the native species, which have been shaped by their environment to be resistant to drought.

All prairie land was born about twenty-five million years ago after the Rocky Mountains were formed. These mountains blocked the flow of moisture-rich air from the Pacific, causing dry conditions east of the range. Few trees grew since the dry land favored grasses. The continental glaciers deposited fine particles of "loess," (ground rock in drifts) and the texture of the minerals supported grass seedlings following the receding of the glaciers.

Unlike trees and shrubs, prairie plant roots and seeds could withstand wildfires. I learned from the brochure that the bur oak was one of the few trees that did not perish in fires, since its thick, corky bark was somewhat resistant to fire. These bur oaks, scattered throughout the prairie region, provided food and shelter for many animal inhabitants.

When the prairie in Willow River was cleared and burned by park employees, stands of big blue stem sprang forth, mingling with clumps of prairie clover, lead plant, and Indian grass. Their seeds had been waiting dormant for years and were suddenly released.

I found a fascinating reference in the brochure about rattlesnake master, a prairie plant in the yucca family, regarding its use by Indians to ease the pain of toothache. I wondered if this rattlesnake master was the same, or related to, the adder's tongue fern prevalent in Asia and Australia.

As the morning progressed, I walked all the way to the abandoned highway I had discovered on an earlier jaunt. One of the park brochures stated that prairie remnants could be discovered along roads and railroad rights-of-way where the grading had not been altered and no herbicides used. Other sources of prairie remnants, according to my guide, were old, little used cemeteries, rocky bluffs and gravelly glacial hills, sand barrens and some large wetland areas.

Luckily the brochure told the novice like myself how to recognize prairie remnants, but I still lacked a basic understanding. I was especially interested in prairie animals and pulled from my pocket another brochure. I knew very little about the prairie world. I was thrilled to learn that bison once may have roamed these very same pastures that I walked, long before the prairie had been converted to farmland. But smaller prairie mammals required less space, and I looked for prairie deer mice, meadow and harvest mice (not that I could tell the difference), moles, shrews, and prairie voles. And, of course, there were thirteen-lined ground squirrels and pocket gophers, both of which I had glimpsed nearly every day since my arrival at Willow River.

The brochure also addressed the question of larger mammals such as cottontail rabbits, red foxes, skunks, weasels,

and badgers. Most interesting, however, was a passage about ornate box turtles. These turtles are among the most ancient of Wisconsin's prairie species and require loose sand on dry prairies to dig nest holes in spring and deep hibernation burrows in fall. Needless to say, if there were any turtles in the area that had not yet gone into hibernation, they did not make themselves visible.

As I examined the roadbed along the abandoned artery, I began to grow hungry and realized that I had spent the entire morning on my prairie nature hike. Sometime after the sun had reached its zenith, I began to cough uncontrollably and became afraid that my on-again-off-again fever was back into on-mode. Although I started in the direction of my campsite, my trek dragged on as I watched birds feeding along the trail and played with the thirteen-lined ground squirrels that zigzagged across my path. Buttons and I even paused once to let a tiny garter snake make its way across our trail into the underbrush. Buttons allowed the reptile to pass only because I was carrying her at the time.

Upon reaching the deserted campground, I opened a can of fruit, made a gourmet sandwich of peanut butter, and broke open a can of barbequed beans, which I toasted on the tiny fire. I rubbed my hands over the blaze to get the chill from my bones both before and after eating. Slowly the blood began to circulate, and I could appreciate the element of fire.

As I sat there by the smoke from the fire thinking about my prairie trek, I recalled several such prairie hikes with my two oldest daughters, Stacy and Stephanie, when they were quite young. The Hennepin County Park Reserve had initiated a system where children could hike designated trails and earn a hiking staff and medallions, and my daughters loved those early morning walks with their dad and the dogs. Upon reaching the halfway point along the trails, we would locate a post where our "tickets" could be stamped as verification of our having hiked and conquered the designated trails. I recalled how the kids often tired on the long treks, but I always refused to carry either of them and insisted that they walk the entire trail if they were to earn a medallion.

The more I thought about it, I wondered why I was always alone with the children and why my wife never accompanied us on any of our wilderness treks. I realized she would never miss her Sunday services, but many times we walked those same trails on Saturday. It seemed I was alone even then but the laughter of my children beside me was the most treasured award anyone could grant me. What I would have given at that moment just to have Stacy and Stephanie as well as Sarah and John beside me. Even if for a moment! I recalled those happy days again when their little feet would romp ahead, each of the girls wanting to be in the lead to proclaim herself the leader of the expedition.

Funny how we take little things like this for granted, thinking life will always be that way, never fluctuating or terminating. I knew better now. I was sure that feeling could never come again, and I wondered about all those people in the world who were yet to be confronted with potential partings. I recalled the days when I coached park-board baseball for John's team—the day he threw a no-hitter, racked up eleven strikeouts, and hit two homeruns. As my mind swirled to different points in the past, I conjured up an image of the many occasions whereupon I served as the wild unbroken stallion that Sarah rode fearlessly across the golden West of our living room carpet.

Another coughing jag interrupted my reverie, and after extinguishing my tiny fire, I picked up Buttons, and we retreated to the semi-warmth of the van. I read for a couple hours but my mind was everywhere but on the book. How could it ever be? I used to think the future was a wonderful place when my four children would graduate from high school and college, marry, raise families, and make numerous pilgrimages to the family home to see mom and dad. Now the future seemed a wasteland for me, a cold, lonely place that would forever be cold and lonely.

I fell asleep with these thoughts. Perhaps tomorrow would be a better day.

20 Tuesday

I did not sleep well last night, partly due to the intense cold but mostly because of my inability to wipe away unpleasant thoughts regarding my divorce situation. I felt not only melancholy but intensely bitter. My wife had always reminded me that bitterness was my worst enemy, and yet this bitterness and I often walked hand in hand through life. In a sense, it seemed that this shadow stalked me more often than not. I have always found life tough, and meeting challenges face to face had not always been easy for me.

Before starting my routine breakfast of cold cereal and even colder bread and butter, my thoughts drifted back twenty years to that damp prison cell in Leavenworth. I recalled my feelings during that particular hell—loneliness, bitterness, fear, and the very realistic belief that there was no hope for any future. I compared my present plight at Willow River to that challenge I struggled to resolve in that tiny, cramped cell and discovered the hurt was quite similar.

At Leavenworth, I was used to waking up wet with my own perspiration, and every morning without fail, I would find nameless green insects crawling all over my body and upon the walls of my cell. It was a horrible way to wake up, and while at first the experience frightened me (not that I could do anything about it), I later learned to merely brush the uninvited hordes away with my hands because I had ceased caring anymore.

Upon awakening in the van, I was not confronted with these hideous green entities, but the same feeling of dread and loneliness was prevalent. Like my life in that cell, I no longer cared to get up that morning. The future was something I would not see or cared to envision. That dreadful sensation of helplessness engulfed me, and I was too tired, too beat up to fight it.

I recalled one horrible evening (or was it morning?) in Leavenworth when I was awakened by a queer scraping sound within my cell. Since prisoners are not permitted clocks, I had no idea what time it was but I knew it was not long until the blast of the 4:00 A.M. work horn sounded. The noise seemed

to emanate from somewhere under my elbow, and my sleepy eyes gazed down at the drawer attached to the base of my bed right next to my extended arm. The drawers were used for storing a prisoner's commodities, namely cigarettes and candy.

I shrieked in terror as my eyes focused on the drawer so near my face and elbow. Hanging on the drawer with its large filthy claws was a hungry rat gnawing away at my Pearson Salted Nut Roll, paper and all. When I screamed, the frightened rat leaped from my bed and dashed out into the shadows of the cellblock, leaving the partially eaten candy bar as a ghastly reminder of its nocturnal visit. I don't know if it was the rat or myself who was the most frightened, but I told myself the rodent could have very easily attacked me rather than have run away.

In the safety of my van at Willow River, I looked around me, almost expecting to see a giant rat parading with a group of winged green insects. Instead, I was greeted only by the very welcome sight of Button's furry head peering out of the sleeping bag. Yet, this latest peril of coping with divorce and nature seemed more devastating than my prison plight. Back then, I was young and could fight back against the elements; now, however, it seemed I neither wished to nor cared. I knew deep inside that I really cared very much, but I would not let myself become aware of this. But whatever defense mechanism I was employing, it wasn't working.

There were no longer any good times that I could foresee. As shattering an experience as that prison had been, there was at least an occasional chuckle. I recalled listening to the prison radio station with my earphones one night, and shortly before the station's midnight closing, they began playing requests. The radio disc jockey, also a prisoner, who was serving time for robbery, read a request for a prisoner who had served time there, been released, and upon another conviction, was sent back to Leavenworth that very day. A group of his friends had requested the song "Welcome Home, Baby" by the Shirelles, and as the song began playing, I could hear soft laughter from several areas in the cellblock.

Now, there could never be a "welcome home, baby" for me. That elusive return to my home and the life I had enjoyed, were, like my prison experience, but a fleeting chapter in my past. I could not help but feel bitter as I tried to eat my breakfast, bitter for my divorce, bitter for having been sent to prison, bitter for having lived. I recollected perhaps the bitterest moment of my life, one that had taken place while I was serving my year of incarceration.

I had been in typing class that fatal afternoon when a guard appeared and summoned me to the prison administrative office. As I entered a small room, I was told to take a seat. A man dressed in a dark blue suit puttered with some paperwork and phone calls before telling me he was the bearer of bad news. I must say I expected the worst, and I was correct in my assumption. Without looking directly at me, the man informed me that my father had passed away a couple days earlier from a heart attack. I asked him why I was not told earlier, and he replied the staff had been very busy. Bureaucracy! I hated it then, and I had always hated it.

The man said nothing else to me nor did he look again in my direction. He merely went back to his mound of paper and pretended to be occupied. There was no signal between the man and any other living being, but after what seemed like an eternity, a guard entered the room and motioned me toward the door.

I was told I did not have to go back to work or typing class for the two hours that remained in the working day. The grim-faced guard returned me to my cell and my agony. I sat for close to two hours with my head in my hands, tears streaming down my face and was still consumed by grief as my fellow prisoners returned to their own cells.

When the four o'clock horn sounded for roll call, I was oblivious to its sound. Each prisoner was required to stand before the barred door in his cell for a head count and every prisoner did as instructed. I was the exception that day. When the guard who counted roll came by my cell, a wide, sadistic grin appeared on his face when he noticed I was not standing.

"Okay, Koblas, you son of a bitch, you'll go to *The Hole* for ten days for this infraction," he bellowed, obviously enjoying his sentence of punishment. I paid him no heed and continued holding my head in the palms of my hands as he walked away gloriously down the tier.

That night, they did not come for me. I was expecting a stay in solitary confinement as the guard had promised, even though I reckoned I deserved no punishment. Morning came but still no trip to *The Hole* and the cold cement bench in the bowels of that wretched castle.

The following afternoon, however, the guard stopped by my cell. For a moment I thought he was partially human, but then I realized there could be no justice behind those prison walls.

"Koblas, when I caught you sitting and ordered you to *The Hole*, I hadn't realized you had just been told your father had died," he stammered. "I am sure you didn't even hear the horn. I am sorry. But you will still have to be punished." He walked away, and I could hear his boot heels echoing down the tier, reminding me of a Nazi soldier strutting victoriously through some hideous concentration camp.

The guard never learned the meaning of compassion. He enjoyed seeing people suffer. I hated him! I always believed I could never hate anyone, but, in all honesty, I hated him. For the next fourteen nights, while other prisoners slept, I had to mop and scrub the guard's cafeteria, then return to work in the morning. I was physically and emotionally drained.

When word was passed through the prisoners' breakfast line a few mornings later that there was a ground-up rat in the oatmeal, I felt that a tiny bit of retribution was being carried out. The cooks in prison were prisoners, not outside personnel, and the guards ate the same food as their captives. Almost no prisoners took oatmeal that morning, but with a smile, I watched the guards gorging themselves. I couldn't see B- from where I was sitting, but I knew he was there, and I knew what he was eating. He didn't!

My wife had told me that it seemed I would never get over my bitterness regarding the prison experience. That bitterness, she said, had been as difficult to deal with for her as it had for me. Perhaps she was right. I would never lose that bitterness for the guard and that whole experience, but I did learn to accept it and live with it. I didn't realize my bitterness ever showed.

Buttons and I climbed back into the van. I was miserable as the dreadful memories continued to haunt me. There would be no reverie that day, nor hikes along the Willow River or along the winding trails of the prairie in search of white quinine. We spent the entire day in the van, Buttons crawling in and out of the sleeping bag and myself brooding over past and present nightmares. I fell asleep in late afternoon and did not awaken until the early hours of the following morning. I was only too thankful that this time there was no morning work horn.

21 Wednesday

Getting up this morning, I was about to step from the van and prepare some breakfast when I noticed Buttons and I had a visitor. A large raccoon, weighing as much as perhaps twenty-five pounds, was foraging through some scraps I had left for the birds.

Raccoons eat the most during the autumn so they can build up their fat reserves for the long winter ahead. I read that during the winter the raccoon often loses up to fifty percent of its own weight. These creatures are omnivorous animals, and their diets change with the seasons and the availability of foods, a diet consisting mainly of nuts, fruits, seeds, insects, frogs, fish, and garbage.

I could not tell if the intruder was male or female, but if this one was of the latter gender, I looked for youngsters accompanying their mother. The racoons mating season fell between January and March. The gestation is sixty-three days long and the mother bears about four young each spring. Baby raccoons begin hunting with their mothers when they are about ten weeks old and then go off on their own when they are thirteen to fourteen months old. No young came to the campsite, however.

Buttons, in seeing we had company, began barking and jumping against the window. Our royal visitor turned his or her head in our direction, seemed to sniff the air, and then continued eating. After a few minutes, it became bored with what it was eating and slowly but graciously scampered off into the woods. Bravely, Buttons jumped from the open door and raced off in pursuit. She returned just in time to join me for a breakfast of bread and peanut butter and some cold cereal.

Today was supply day, and following our anything-but-hot meal, we drove into Hudson and bought groceries. While paying for our fare, I talked with a young female clerk who told me that snow was in the forecast. I still was not feeling well—my fever had waxed and waned over several days and my cough refused to abate. I considered buying some additional clothing but I had to watch my money, and what I had taken with me would have to suffice. I was more than grateful to my brother-in-law Charlie for giving me two thermal insulated shirts that I slept in each night.

I took a short hike down Walnut Street and let the wind blow me toward the river. Standing on the levee, I realized there were few people about as Buttons charged a group of feeding geese that had forgotten to fly south. I walked in the direction of the Interstate Bridge that connected Wisconsin and Minnesota. After some time, I reversed direction and began walking out on a causeway that jetted out into the river. I assumed I could walk to the Minnesota side of the river but the isthmus terminated long before I could step upon Minnesota soil.

My dog and I walked back toward downtown Hudson, and the buildings constituting its miniature skyline seemed more and more like home to me. I thought of dropping in at the newspaper office but instead marched into a local café and ate a hot meal. Buttons, of course, had to wait in the van but she didn't seem to mind. Her tiny legs were tired after our long walk, and I think she was grateful to escape the piercing wind.

Following lunch, we drove up the steep hill at Birkmose Park, revisited the Indian mounds and took in the breathtaking scenery. I tried to pinpoint where we had walked on the causeway and I thought our route was visible from where I was standing.

Driving back down the hill, I drove to the historic Octagon House that was built in 1855 for Judge John Shaw Moffat and his wife, Nancy. The Moffats had arrived in Hudson in 1854 with their daughter Mary after having lived in New York. The door, however, was locked, and I was not surprised the museum was closed for the season although the brochure in my pocket stated the house was open through October.

I walked around the back of the odd-shaped house to gaze at the blacksmith shop and garden house, but like my own former dwelling in Minneapolis, I was merely on the outside looking in.

Standing in front of the Octagon House, I looked across the street at the also historic Phipps Inn, which was considered the "grand Dame" of Hudson's Victorian houses. Built in 1887, the Phipps was very attractive, and I was drawn to its lead glass windows and elegant furnishings that were visible to the passerby.

Just down the street, I paused in front of the plush Jefferson Day House at 1109 Third Street. Walking back to my van, I drove back the way I had come along the historic district's fashionable Third Street and stopped in front of 727, the Boyden House. For a time, I was lost in the nineteenth century, and, for those few moments, I had forgotten about my own terrible state. Then reality swept over me with a wave of nausea, and I drove away from Hudson.

Back at the campsite, I took out my copy of Henry Beston's *The Outermost House* and attempted to lose myself again, this time in Beston's observation of the monarch butterfly:

"Their movements were as casual as the wind, yet there was an unmistakable southerly pull drawing them on," wrote Beston. "I imagine they were in search of food. Between half-past twelve and half-past one, they melted away as mysteriously as they had come, and with them went the last echo of summer and the high sun from the dunes."

I could not help but think about my own senseless plight. Instead of immersing myself in Beston's world of nature on the seashore at Cape Cod, I found I could not project myself away from my predicament. My own life, too, had melted away mysteriously and with it the last echo of summer. Ahead lay only the long, cold winter and a lifetime of loneliness. I am not a drinking man, but I think if I had had liquor with me at that moment, I would have become one. Instead I lay back on the seat and closed my eyes in an attempt to drown out the world about me. Sleep, however, did not come for several hours. I was plagued by a series of coughs, and the cold wind that penetrated the windows was much too much to bear. When I did manage to find the arms of Morpheus, I did so only sporadically, and was awake most of the night.

No headlights shone on my window; I knew no one was coming, and I resigned myself to my fate.

22 Thursday

I did not feel like eating breakfast this morning. I was cold, sick, and utterly depressed. I did manage to open a can of dog food for Buttons, but the cold wind sent me back to the sanctuary of the van. I knew the day would be a bad one, and I would not be able to cope with my situation. For a while I sat watching for "her," she, who could drive up at any moment, take my hand, and take me home. Still, I knew this was not to be, not today or any other.

I don't know why, but my thoughts went back to my childhood. I recalled those terrors of childhood as vividly as if they were confronting me now. I recalled the man from City Hall, a "servant of the people," talking with my father in our living room on Fifth Street. My dad had purchased nearly a city block of run-down business dwellings, and since he was a carpenter, he planned on restoring the block. He would rent the downstairs portion of each building to various businessmen and the upstairs apartments to interested residents. He himself planned to open a beer tavern in the choicest spot.

The politician told my father "they" did not want him to open a tavern on Cedar Avenue and advised him he would be much better off running a grocery store at that location. But my father did not want a grocery store and was adamant about operating the tavern. I peered through the door at the chalk-white face of the City Hall man, and I was frightened of him. When he finally left, he was very angry, and I did not fully understand what I had overheard and witnessed.

Within a few weeks we began receiving live bullets in the mail, disguised in carefully wrapped packaging. I wondered who could send us bullets and why would they do so. More bullets came, but my father became even more adamant about starting his tavern business.

Then, on two occasions, my father's large plate glass window at the tavern he was about to open was smashed to pieces during the night. As young as I was, I began to put the pieces of the jigsaw together and was aware that someone did not want that tavern to open. It finally did, though, nonetheless.

Shortly thereafter, I, and not my father, began getting threatening phone calls from voices I could not recognize. They were the voices of grown men, not always the same one, but each and every call was threatening. They knew my name, "Jackie," and said they were going to kill me. I was but eleven-years old and could not understand what I had done to warrant such threats.

One day a blue car began following me home from school. I was terrified and ran between some houses, thinking I had escaped to the opposite side of the block. I did in fact emerge on the next block but so did the blue car that had taken the alley and intercepted me. Again I ran, and ran, until the blue car was gone.

More often than not, I walked home from school with a little neighbor girl, my friend Julie. We were walking home from school through an alley just north of Franklin Avenue in Minneapolis when I noticed three men standing by a parked car behind a bar. One of them yelled, "Jackie, come here. We are friends of your brother." I was suspicious, but still I slowly shuffled toward the car. The same man said, "Jackie, there is someone in the car who wants to see you."

I stopped short of the back of the car. My brain began to flash danger signals, and it did not take a scholar to realize that if I approached the car door, I would be trapped between the car, the building, and the men. I screamed at the top of my lungs, "Run, Julie, it's a trap," and the two of us fled down the alley. The three men who had been standing by the car began to run after us, but once we reached the street, they turned back. I don't think Julie and I stopped running until we reached home.

My father then called the police. The phone calls were still coming but tracing devices were not very effective in the early 1950s. I even recalled being driven to school a couple times by police detectives. However, most of my fear did not surface at school while in the company of schoolmates.

It was the phone calls that terrified me. Many of them would be late at night when my mother had left to pick up my father. The calls were always timed perfectly, and I had little doubt "they" were watching the house from the deep shadows of the Catholic church next door.

One night my mother had to be gone awhile to help my father close up the tavern. From what I could remember, an employee had called in sick, and my father was short-staffed. Shortly after my mother left, the telephone rang. With a trembling hand, I picked up the receiver and said hello. The voice on the other end was straight out of a horror movie, and I had all I could do to stay on my feet when it bellowed, "I know you are home alone tonight, Jackie. I am watching the house and will be there to get you in a couple minutes. And this time I am going to slit your throat and chop you into pieces."

When he hung up, I quickly dialed the number at my parents' tavern only to get a busy signal. I recalled only recently listening to the radio broadcast of "Sorry, Wrong Number," and those horrors of that situation were not so unlike my own. Again I dialed the number and again the same busy signal.

I raced to the porch and looked out at the church wall. A parade of grotesque beings waltzed in and out of the bushes

before my eyes, and I had to squeeze my hands to keep them from shaking. A car went by, and with it shadows played on the brick of the old church, and I raced to the back door and peered out to see if my attacker was coming from that direction.

I nearly fainted when I heard the front doorbell ring. Slowly advancing to the door, all the while swearing I would never open it, I peered through the bottom blind at a man's shoes and Khaki pants. I lifted another blind a little higher up and still another, seeing a man's shirt and two muscular arms. I hesitated before opening the next blind, the one that would reveal the ghastly face of my antagonist.

When I did, I began to cry. Standing at the door was my Uncle Yano who lived across the street. He said my parents had called and asked him to check on me. I told him of the horror that had just transpired, and he hugged me like he never had before. Then he walked out front looking for any would-be intruder. God, but I loved him at that moment.

But this night was not to be the most terrifying of all. As the calls kept coming, the voice on the other end kept asking me to meet with him and talk things over. A detective was in our home during one of these sessions listening in on another phone he had brought with him and attached to ours. He instructed me that the next time the ogre called, I should tell him I would meet him at such and such a time at a local drugstore. When the man did call back, I set up the trap for seven o'clock the next evening.

Still, I kept asking myself if the man could be that stupid to show up, knowing that police would be all over the building. But on the phone, the caller showed no anxiety and said he would be there. He then made me promise that I would too.

The following night, my father and I sat in an unmarked police car around the corner from the drugstore. The detective told me to go in and just hang out for an hour. He said I did not have to be afraid because his men would be in and out of the store dressed in plain clothes and that I would never be alone. I would not know who they were because I would not be able to recognize them, but help would be there. Plus, the police had informed the druggist of the plot, and so the hour would be a very safe one.

As I entered the drugstore, I wanted to turn and run and never stop running. But the detective had assured me that I would be safe. Walking through the store, I paused and perused several items on the shelves, trying not to appear suspicious. I became frightened, though, when I discovered I was the only "customer" in the store.

A chilling thought suddenly manifest. How was I to identify the bad guys from the police? They would all look the same, I would have no way of knowing who any of the intruders would be whether I should move toward or away from them during the confrontation.

A man dressed in a long gray coat with a dress hat pulled slightly over one eye entered the aisle and began looking at merchandise about ten to fifteen feet away. I kept telling myself he must be one of the detectives, but then I asked myself if he could be the killer.

I almost screamed and darted from the store but somehow I kept my cool. When a woman strode into the next aisle, I walked in her direction as if she were my mother. I felt safe standing near her and wished I could hug her. Then a thought frightened me away from her. How did I know she wasn't in on it with them, as she would provide the gang with a ruse in her role of a disinterested housewife? After all, the police would not be looking for a woman. I turned warily into a different aisle and pretended to be studying a different set of merchandise.

Throughout that miserable hour, other men, also wearing hats, entered the drugstore and walked by my aisle. Again, I wondered if these men were members of the police force or members of the gang. I trusted no one, and I was relieved when I saw the woman leave the store.

When no one was in the store, I felt abandoned and wondered what would happen if the real criminal or criminals entered with no one present to protect me. Still, I liked it better when no one was in the store because all those men with hats looked at me and each and every one of them frightened me. Theoretically, the detectives watched me because they aimed to protect me, but the others, if present, watched too for a different reason.

The long hour, which seemed like two, comprised the most frightening ordeal of my young life. If the evil man came to the store, he did not reveal his identity. I was relieved when the detective, whom I recognized, came in with my father and said it was all over, and I could go home. I remember thanking him but told him I would never be a set up again, and I meant it. It took me years to get over that awful incident if I ever did at all and I think the slight tremor I have today was caused by that night of horror.

The calls kept coming for another month or two. Then one night, the caller apologized for terrorizing my family and me, and said they never would bother us again. I think they kept their word too, but I would never recover from the nervous strain they placed upon me.

Buttons' bark brought me back to the present with a startle. A small squirrel was doing acrobatics on our picnic table outside the van, and I let my canine out to challenge the intruder. The confrontation lasted but seconds, as the squirrel, faced with a "superior force," scampered up a tree much to Buttons' dismay. Then I called her back to the van.

I don't think I ate anything all day. I slept on and off throughout the afternoon and sat up only when the coughing seizures prevented my lying horizontally. I felt much worse than the day before, both physically and mentally, and I didn't care about anything transpiring outside the van. For the first night since I had come to Willow River, I did not look for those headlights. They weren't coming anyway, and why should they? She, that woman—my wife—seemed as distant just then as those childhood memories of a frightened little boy in a drugstore a long, long time before.

23 Friday

I was up early this morning, and after a hastily eaten breakfast, I drove to the Hidden Ponds Trail. Buttons raced far ahead of me as we started along the billowing Prairie Sea, but she would always stop and make sure I was following.

I carried in my hand a brochure that bore a picture of a black cherry. The fruit of the black cherry is often used to make a delicious jelly, although one has to be very careful not to include the pits, leaves or stems when making preserves. These parts of the black cherry contain hydrogen cyanide, a very deadly poison. I decided, however, the jelly was not all that important and was frightened away by the warning of the deadly poison.

I removed a small bag from my jacket pocket and began picking up hazelnuts from the ground. These nuts from the wild filbert have a sweet nut flavor, although most of them had ripened in August and September. Still, I gathered several to feed the squirrels and spent most of the morning looking for hazelnuts.

Late in the morning, I paused before a basswood and read my brochure. According to the printed guide, every part of the basswood has a useful purpose. In winter the bright red buds are eaten as survival food, and I began to shudder, wondering how long before I would be tackling the buds. In the spring, young leaves are often used in salads, and the blossoms, dried, are used for tea. Bees make honey from these very same blossoms, and people use the young fruit as beans or peas. The ripe fruits can also be roasted, ground and used as a substitute for chocolate. American Indians, for rope and basket-making, used the inner bark of the basswood and the soft wood can be used for many purposes, including the making of piano keys.

After filling my bags as well as pockets with hazelnuts, Buttons and I returned to the van along the trail. The wind was nippy, and my face felt raw as the cold seeped mercilessly into my pores. I sat in the van for a couple hours reading Henry Beston's *The Outermost House*, for probably the third or fourth time. I could feel the loneliness of Beston's winter beach, but I also was aware that the author could go home to his wife and a hot meal at any time.

It must have been close to four o'clock in the afternoon when I made a sandwich for Buttons and me, then snuggled into the seat of the van. I turned on the engine and let the heat warm the van for nearly twenty minutes, then shut it down, and began the process of freezing once again. I noticed Buttons had already slipped into my sleeping bag, but I was not ready to sleep.

After a while, I drove onto the road that formed the backbone of Willow River State Park and began looking for deer. It was already getting dark, but after two or three sweeps both ways through the park, I counted eighteen deer. Once I stepped from the van and cautiously approached two of the deer, but they fled before I could get halfway up the hill.

I had the urge to drive back into Hudson, but since I had all the supplies I needed for a few days, the journey was unnecessary. I was bored! I could think about home and my beloved wife to break the spell of boredom, but that would only make me crazy again. I preferred the boredom.

I didn't eat any supper that evening. I was still reasoning that if I ate but twice a day rather than the customary three meals, I could conserve my money and make it last several days longer. I knew this was not doing my body any good, especially with the cough and fever, but it was a rule I had decided to live by. Besides, I was a little overweight anyway and needed to shed a few pounds.

I went to sleep thinking about my wife and four children, trying to guess what each of them might be doing at that very moment. Again, I wondered if any of them were thinking of me. My eyes were fixed on the narrow road that meandered through the campground, and I entertained visions of the children jumping out of the car as it drove up to rescue me. There were no children, no wife, nor the car that night, but I imagined it happening with all my will and even managed a smile for a couple minutes. Then I was lost in dream.

24 Saturday

John came up early this morning with my friend Mike. Now, Mike is a fisherman and the most devoted angler I have ever known. Mike used to come over quite often during my days of bliss in Minneapolis with my family and he would always tell John stories of his fishing exploits. I don't know how many of them were embellished, but like a hungry walleye, John was hooked. Mike took John with him on a couple of his fishing trips, and John enjoyed himself to no end, whether they caught a string of fish or not. With Mike, it was always catch and release. Mike didn't fish to eat but did so for the joy of angling. He respected the adventure much more than the prize.

I was ecstatic when they handed me a bag of real hot food from the seat in Mike's truck. "Hurry up and eat," Mike demanded. "We need to go to the bait shop and then get some fish." I hurried through my breakfast, sharing parts of it with Buttons, who was only too anxious to help me finish the meal quickly.

We were off to the bait shop in Burkhardt where Mike engaged in "fish talk" with the man behind the counter, a jargon consisting of such foreign sounding terms as Rappellas, jigs, and such. I have never been a fisherman so I paid little attention to the strange conversation. John did, however, and I realized that my son was steeped in this foreign language almost as much as Mike.

Driving to the Upper Falls, the three of us climbed down the trail to a spot below the falls that Mike had divined as a good one. Within seconds, John and Mike had lines in the water and the latter began wading into the stream. I asked him what he planned on catching and he answered, "Eelpouts!" I had no idea what an eelpout was, and I wondered if Mike was joking with me.

Mike attempted to explain that there were about eighty species of eelpout and they were usually found in the cold waters of Arctic and Antarctic regions. These thick-lipped fish, at least the saltwater variety, often reached a length of up to three feet. The eelpouts he was fishing for were quite different and not much larger than a minnow. These fish that are often used as bait lived on the bottom of the rivers in Wisconsin and seemed to prefer shallow water.

Both fishermen landed some small trout and released them immediately. We spent several hours at the falls before moving to another spot nearer the campground. Their luck was not as good here but neither of them seemed to mind. As they fished away the afternoon, I climbed the hill and made some sandwiches.

Following our late lunch, the three of us hiked along the Willow Falls Trail. The woods mesmerized Mike, but he always kept an eye on the stream we were following. Every once in a while he would point at a certain point along the trail and express an interest in fishing there later. Buttons left us a couple times to chase birds and squirrels, but she always seemed to know exactly where we were.

In reaching the falls, I asked Mike if he considered them beautiful. He said he did, but I noticed his eyes were fixed on the water below. I knew then that he was oblivious to everything around him if there was a potential fishing site nearby. I told him what I suspected about his eye for beauty. He chuckled and said I might be right. Now this was dedication!

This was one of the better days I spent at Willow River. Mike has a good sense of humor and was able to make me laugh several times. My son, John, was with me, and he had plenty of stories about my daughters Stacy, Stephanie, and Sarah. I felt that the girls were with me too, at least their thoughts and their hearts.

Following our nightly drive to search for deer, Mike was astonished to find thirty-seven of them in less than an hour. Although he had to leave for Minneapolis, John was staying with me for another night and day. Mike left us standing in the dark campground, but not before promising he would be back for another visit soon. I hated to see him go. The whole world had not abandoned me, and the joint laughter had really given me a boost.

I looked at John nearly asleep on the back seat. God, how I loved him and my three daughters back home. Their

home, that is! I wanted to tell John how much I cared about my children, but I was at a loss for words, and he was already asleep. I drank a can of pop and let Buttons out to do her business. Tomorrow would be another wonderful day!

25 Sunday

We were up early and hiking along the Willow Falls Trail. John seemed to not be bothered by the cold and walked at a pretty fast pace. I tried to keep up with him and a couple times asked him to slow down. When we reached the falls, we sat for nearly an hour and admired their beauty. John then raced up the steep hill that I always had trouble ascending and I followed. Several times I stopped to rest and attempted to catch my breath. It became obvious, however, that no matter how long I rested, I was still gasping for air. A combination of a steep hill and old age. John, however, did not stop to rest once.

I remembered that not long ago I possessed nearly his stamina and could even outrun him. Well, sort of! When the kids were little, they had decided to take the old eight-millimeter movie camera out of the closet and make their own film, "Jungle Bob's Adventure." And of course, in true movie spirit, there was a sequel, "Jungle Bob in Alaska." Since Stacy paid for the films, it came as no surprise that she directed them, starred in them (do I have to add?), produced them, chose the site locations and the props, and pretty much dictated who would play each part.

The director had even planned a third film—"Jungle Bob Goes to Mars"—but those plans were scratched when the villain's costume, a giant-beaked black Magpie suit, was torn to shreds during a thrilling action sequence that featured a sordid fist fight in a cave. The Magpie, however, did serve the purpose in the two films that did see the light of day.

John, of course, was Jungle Bob—the fearless hero of the cinema. His girlfriend—the heroine, named Melanie

Goldsmith—was played by Stephanie. Sarah was too little to accompany us, but she was with us in spirit. I drove the kids to several locations for footage. I had to remind Stacy that she could not shoot the film if she were starring in it as well and managed to take the camera from her part of the time. Stacy had chosen me for the role of the villain, and I had to chase Jungle Bob and Melanie all through the never-ending three-minute film. I had great speed for my age and was surprised that I could overtake even John at short distances.

Not so at Willow River! He was standing, not sitting, on top of the bluff when I reached the summit. "Come on, dad," he grumbled, and I followed, too windless to answer. At the Scott homestead, I finally managed to talk him into a few minutes respite, but he was soon on his feet and marching down the path. Jungle Bob was in his prime, and I had certainly lost any spark that once glowed, within or without.

In the afternoon, John fished below the campsite while I read. He didn't catch many fish, but he was having a ball. John asked if I wanted to live here permanently so he could come up every weekend and enjoy it with me. And, of course, there was no school in summer, and he could stay with me for the season. As much as I love the forests, valleys, and water, I declined his proposal, since staying through summer would mean enduring the onslaught of winter as well. I did convey to him, however, that we could come up to Willow River almost any time we wanted.

In the evening, I drove John back to Minneapolis. John did not see my face as we rode along but tears were streaming down my cheeks. Perhaps he did and was too polite to say so. I had always fancied myself as having a rugged exterior—a person who seldom showed pain and almost never anguish—but since my retreat to Willow River, never a day went by that I didn't cry.

I was rewarded by hugs from Stacy, Stephanie, and Sarah and even Cassie as I walked John up to the door to his home. I could see my wife doing dishes in the kitchen. Once, she looked at me and then turned away. She was content with this life, I could tell. I don't think she missed me at all, and I felt like a stranger at the doorstep of my own home. I wanted to cry out a greeting, but I knew that there would be no response. I told the four kids I loved them and climbed back into the van. I began to cry as I saw their pretty noses pressed against the window and forced a smile in response to their waving hands. But I could see the agony in their faces, too. They could hide their sorrows better than I, even though I was the adult.

I did not look back as I left the driveway and entered the street. I could feel their love through the window, and I knew they were straining for a look at their father as I approached the corner. I simply could not let them see my anguish!

26 Monday

The ranger stopped by early this morning to inquire about my health. Since I am the only camper here at Willow River these days, I seem to get very special attention. I informed the ranger I was not feeling too badly although my cough had escalated. I also told him I would be leaving on the first of the month and thought I would be fine up through that time. Still, he was very concerned, and we talked for about twenty minutes.

I looked over Sarah's letter this morning after the ranger left. Seven years old and away from her daddy! I had trouble with that stark realization, and I missed her more than ever. My thoughts went out to Stacy and Stephanie, too, and John, and my mother, and, of course, my wife. Today would be another empty day—John was not coming, and Mike would not be there with his fishing pole. I wondered about Dodo too and what he was doing.

The morning was very cold, and I knew that below-zero temperatures were just around the corner. So far I had been lucky that the snow flurries did not settle upon the ground during my stay. I suppose I had lied to the ranger about my health as I was feeling anything but good. My temperature was raging and for now, refusing to go away. My cough was as active as ever, and I perspired even though the temperatures were very cool. I did not feel like eating or walking the Willow Falls Trail. Even reading was becoming difficult to enjoy, and I was content to just sit in the van and close my eyes.

Of course, Buttons needed my attention. I made sure she was fed and warm, and on several occasions, took her for short hikes through the deserted campground. It seemed so lonely with no one else occupying the other sites, but in my own way, I liked it this way. The cold wind blew leaves against my legs as we walked, and I tightened my scarf around my neck. Buttons was wearing her little red woolen sweater—a turtleneck.

A squirrel dashed across our path during one of these brief excursions, and, as always, Buttons took off for the chase. I don't know what she would have done had she caught her quarry, for the squirrel was as large as she. But with so many trees about, this could never happen.

I thought about the many birthday parties Stacy and Stephanie had enjoyed, and how I had planned each and every one of them the best I could. All the neighbor kids always came, my mother made a cake or I bought one, and the happiest sound of all—the laughter of children—echoed from our yard. Poor Sarah had never enjoyed a birthday party. Her mother's religion forbade such occasions, and my little one was afraid to go against her mother's wishes. I wished at that moment I could give her a special party, but I wondered now that I was gone if she would ever be the recipient of such a festive gathering.

I think I missed my four children most of all. We had always been so close, but I knew, no matter what, that bond could never be broken. I saw before me those pretty faces pressed against the window only last night, and I had trouble controlling the tears that began to drip down my cheeks.

"Get yourself together, man," a voice inside me ordered and I dried my eyes with my coat sleeve. Sometimes it felt good to cry.

When I went to bed, I could not sleep. The coughing fits were really getting serious, and I had little doubt I was experiencing another bout with either bronchitis or pneumonia. I was tempted to give up my stay and drive into Minneapolis and see a doctor. Yet, I had come so close to a full month at Willow River that I could not abandon my plan. If I had to spend my final week in the van hacking away, then it would be so.

27 Tuesday

I was asleep in my bed, thank God, my wife next to me, when I heard the bedroom door open. Straining to see through the piercing blackness, I saw a young man entering the room. I sat up abruptly, for the boy entering the room had no head. Beneath his arm he carried that missing head, and I clutched my wife's hand as the sinister form shambled to the bedside.

"I'm going to make a run for it. I can't stand it, I have to run," reverberated words from the emptiness where a head should be. With one arm around my wife, I screamed as never before, and the figure vanished into the darkness.

I looked around me. The boy was gone, and I was no longer in my bedroom. Instead, I was sitting up in my van in the woods of Willow River. I had been dreaming again, but yet this time, it seemed so real. Even though I realized it had been a dream, I looked about the van to see—hoping, hoping—if my wife were really with me.

"Damn dream," I muttered to myself, checking to see if Buttons was okay. It was just getting light and I could swear I hadn't slept a wink all through the night. The cough never left me, and several times during the night, I had to sit up and turn on the engine for some heat. Whenever I went through this exercise, I had to make sure I stayed awake while the engine was running, as I was very aware of the consequences.

Not only was I afraid of running out of gas, but I was also on the lookout for any would-be carbon monoxide leakage.

I longed to walk the Willow Falls Trail but today would be like the one before and I would be unable to leave the van for any real length of time. Finally, I decided to drive into Hudson and purchase some cough medicine and various cold remedies. I think I was in town for all of ten minutes, before speeding back along the road to Willow River. I was glad to be back "home" and I immediately went to sleep in the middle of the day.

When I was finally awakened by another series of coughing, it was already getting dark. I opened another can of dog food for Buttons and stretched back out on the seat. I noticed my body was visibly trembling, a combination of the cold and my illness. Still, I was able to fall back asleep and there were no severed heads this time to disturb my slumber.

28 Wednesday

I was up early. Since I had eaten almost nothing the past two days, I decided I had to get some food in me. I was not hungry, nor was I even thirsty. Taking a piece of nearly frozen bread from the van, I smeared a heavy dose of peanut butter across its surface and forced myself to eat it. My fever had not left me; neither had the cough.

I would force myself to get some exercise as well, and Buttons and I set off down the Willow Falls Trail. There is a sharp bend along the trail where the path dips into a valley, and I found myself pausing halfway down the descent. I had no desire to climb any hills today and wisely turned around at this point before committing myself any further down the gradual slope.

Buttons, however, was far down the incline, and since I have never been able to whistle, I began shouting her name. For a moment, I feared she had gotten lost, but all of a sudden, she darted out from the bushes and nearly knocked me over.

Upon reaching the campsite, I saw the ranger's truck parked there. He was again checking on my well-being and I assured him I was doing fine. Hoarseness in my throat betrayed me, however, and he told me I really should drive into Hudson for medical treatment. I said I would think about it, but didn't feel my condition was anything to worry about.

The ranger brought me a new park trail map, and although it was not much different than the wrinkled version I carried in my jacket, I longed to hike the trails all over again once my health improved. He asked if I was keeping up with my journal, and I produced the notebook and let him read a couple entries. He told me I was a very dedicated man, and I replied that I was also a very foolish one.

Following his leave, I went back into the van and slept for a couple hours. Upon awakening, I combed my hair in the rear view mirror and laughed over the length of my beard. I hadn't shaved in a month, and I fancied I appeared little different from many of the creatures I shared a forest with at Willow River. The long beard, however, helped keep my neck warm, and I vowed to let shaving go until my return to "civilization."

I thought about my friends—Wally, Russell, Steve, Andy, Doc, Dave, Joe—and decided to call them once I was back in Minneapolis. After all, almost no one knew where I had gone, and yet, I found it difficult to even consider speaking to anyone, friend or foe. The healing process would take a long time, and perhaps the emotional wounds I had endured would never heal. Life is like that, I guess, only we never realize this until we are lost amidst the calamity.

My thoughts, too, were of my mentor, Donald Wandrei, who lived in his cluttered house in St. Paul with piles of books and manuscripts. We had talked nearly every day over the past fifteen years, and I was certain Don was worrying about me. Two of the books I had with me were written by Wandrei—*Strange Harvest* and *The Web of Easter Island,* and I pulled them from one of the boxes in the rear of the van and began paging through them. I had read both at least twice but I thought of my friend, who like myself, was an outsider.

Don had taught me that writing was a lonely life. I guess I knew that when I had begun my quest for publication, but not even this brand of loneliness had prepared me for Willow River. I decided Don would be one of the first persons I contacted when I left my self-imposed isolation. Don would know what to do. He always knew what to do.

I spent nearly an hour shifting boxes from one side of the van to the very back in an attempt to cover every possible crack where wind could find even the slightest entry. I don't know if this exercise did any good but at least it kept me occupied and somewhat warm.

I did not eat again that day nor did I venture back out along the trail with Buttons. I began reading over some of the passages in the Wandrei books and, when darkness fell, put them aside and fell asleep. For a couple moments I was home again by the warm fireplace with my family.

29 Thursday

Very cold this morning. The van was running most of the night in my feeble attempt to get warm. Now if only the snow would hold out. Feeling very much under the weather this morning. I did manage to eat a bowl of cereal, or most of it, and drank some orange juice. No trail walks today, no drives into town, not even a stroll through the deserted campground.

I looked over a couple booklets I had purchased at the newspaper office in Hudson to kill some time and wrapped Buttons and myself in blankets. It was a long, depressing day, not unlike most of the others, and my memories flashed before me like a moving picture show. I drank several cans of diet cola to prevent dehydration and snacked on a few stale potato chips I had purchased in one of my earlier trips into Hudson.

Just before retiring for the night, I took a book of poetry from one of the boxes and sought beauty in despair. I fell asleep with the book on my shoulder and Buttons in my lap.

30 Friday

In a sense, I was relieved that my stay at Willow River was about to end. It was cold, I was ill, and I wanted to see all my children. Still, I had become accustomed to the place and each tree, every dale, each bend of the river, and the beautiful trails that wind endlessly through the forests and across the prairie had become friends. We had established a kinship, and as ludicrous as it might seem to an outsider, I almost felt as if the wilds of Willow River understood my pain.

There would be no more hiking the Willow Falls Trail, no observation of deer at dusk, and no more absolute solitude. In a few days I would be lost in the mainstream of human society—the bustling, dead-end chaos that binds us all. I was not anxious to return to that, yet I knew I must. I felt as if Buttons could tell we were leaving soon as well, and the stark reality of losing the forest and prairie left me with an undeniable emptiness. This is not quite valid, however, as this very same emptiness had taken possession before I had come to Willow River. Perhaps I was experiencing the loss of my sanctuary. Here in the woods I was free to feel sorry for myself, to weep if I wanted or to resign myself to misery. I was never criticized here, and I was that four-year-old kid again, talking to "live" wooden toys that I had created and marched through the neighborhood.

Tomorrow then would be my last full day at Willow River and I racked my tired brain about preparations, making a mental list of all the things I had to do before I left. The list was not necessary, however, as there were no preparations. I was free—yes, freer than I even wanted to be—but when the time came, all I had to do was drive away. There would be no tearful good-byes, no fanfare, and no one would notice my absence. There would simply be just one more vacant spot in the campground and that emptiness would be complete.

Buttons and I stayed close to the van all day. Twice we started up the Willow Falls Trail but both times turned around after walking but a hundred yards. I ate little and coughed a lot. Reading helped pass the time, but I found I could only peruse so many pages and would have to close the book and nap. When evening came, my dog and I were both chilled to the bone, and I knew that the coming night would not be one of sleep. The motor ran more than it was off throughout the night, and it was so dark I could barely see beyond my hand.

31 Saturday

I awakened early and drove into Hudson for a hot meal. I really in all honesty was not very hungry, despite my lack of nourishment the past few days, but I knew the drive would warm up the van and its two occupants. John had wanted to come up for my last day at Willow, but I asked him to stay at home as I would be coming to see him the following day. It would have been nice having John with me, but I felt I needed the time to reflect on my situation and whether I had accomplished anything by staying in the woods for an entire month.

If my experience had taught me anything, it had instilled a strong will to survive. I was but a shell of a man when I had arrived here one month earlier, and although I hate to admit it, perhaps a little suicidal. Willow River, however, taught me to live with my pain, to go on and try to deal with it. Of course, I would always be looking back, but it was okay to sometimes look back. That, no one could take away from me. The pain would always be there, better on some days and worse on others, but I would find a way to deal with it.

When the waitress in the cafe took my order, I felt as if I had been away for years. But, too, I wondered if I had ever really left. I wondered too if this young lady or anyone in that restaurant took their lives for granted. I almost wanted to mount a soapbox and preach to the world about what I had learned. Instead I ate my meal quietly and decided to live a peaceful coexistence with the world.

Driving to the top of Birkmose Park, I stood by a mound and took a final glimpse at the awe-inspiring beauty of the St. Croix Valley. Minnesota beckoned from across the river, and when the two or three people in the park were not looking, I waved at the Gopher State. I did not stay out of the van for long, however, as the piercing wind swept the bluffs and everything in its way. I began to wonder how we had survived at all for an entire month, but I was not sorry for my retreat to this other world.

Upon returning to Willow River State Park, I stopped at the office and informed the rangers that I would be leaving in the morning. They were glad to see me going, and although they insisted they would miss my company, they declared an attempt to stay on would only jeopardize my health.

The wind was biting through my skin, kicking up the leaves and twigs by the time we reached the campground and "old #28." I spent the afternoon lost in a book of poetry. Many of the poems reminded me of my wife and the lost love verse bit deeply into my heart. But I did not close the book and I did not let myself fall to pieces as I may have a few nights earlier. I was, after all, going back into the world. I had no idea where I was going or how I would live, but there is something sacred in a return to normalcy whether I functioned as an observer or became a part of it.

There was no fear of returning to the city with but cents in my pocket. I had family and friends on whom I could lean if that was what I needed. But it was much more than that. Although I had no direction, I now had discovered who I was and what I was and was not capable of achieving. Too, if things did not pan out, I could always turn back toward Willow River, although any attempt at surviving the winter would be futile.

I spent my last night in the woods thinking of my wife, my children, and a shallow future. I was not afraid of the many tomorrows but wondered only if my constitution was strong enough to cope with a pain that would never end. I would miss Willow River as a friend who would always be there for me. Part of me—my heart and discarded pain—would remain, and if there were anything to this business of a soul, my psychic residue would be left behind there for years to come.

When I closed my eyes to sleep, I fancied I had just turned out the light as I had done so many times at home. My last thought before falling into oblivion was of a pretty and gentle face smiling at me from a long white wedding gown. As my bride of twenty years stepped towards me with outstretched hands, I fell into her arms and all the world went away.

The Beginning

It is a different October now as I sit on a hill overlooking Willow Falls. Twelve years have passed since Buttons and I went to live there during a time of great upheaval in my life. I sit with a different dog now—Licorice—as my beloved Buttons passed away earlier this summer. This is not the same Willow River where I once went to sort out my dreams and fears and endure a pain I was unable to come to grips with. The dams at the upper and middle falls have been razed, a change, I suppose for the good, restoring the river to its natural state. Work has been done on many of the trails—Willow Falls Trail is closed temporarily for restoration—and even my old campsite number twenty-eight no longer bears the same number. The numbers of each campsite were changed some time after I left Willow River in 1987, and I am not sure which site was once mine. A nature center has even been constructed near the Hidden Ponds Trail base.

Buttons and I pulled out of Willow River early in the morning of November 1, 1987, just as the snows swept down into the valleys, blanketing the trees and prairies in a white kimono. One of my first stops was the office of a physician where my pneumonia was confirmed. That illness was curable, but the everlasting hurt, my own bereavement of the soul, was not. My pain was not to go away, but still, my retreat into the depths of Willow River taught me how to deal with that hurt and to accept it. Many have gone before me, and there shall be many more to follow. Wisdom is not an attribute many of us humans are blessed with, and although I fancy myself a writer, I never was able to communicate during those dark days of autumn.

Would I do it again, that is, if faced with the failure of a marriage, would I return to the solitude of a Willow River? I think so, although I am no longer the young man I was. There is a certain elixir about the woods—its solitude mends a broken heart and restores faith in life—and I could never find that peace anywhere else. Yes, I would go back and lose myself among those willows and cottonwoods, dream my dreams that could not come true, and again watch for those headlights that never came.

I find myself a stranger here now—a man who comes to study beauty but who is afraid to look deep within his own soul. Still, Willow River will always hold a very special place in my heart, and when I close my eyes and concentrate, I can almost hear the woods stir and come alive. As my thoughts go out to the forest, again I hear echoing through the river valley, the sobs of a displaced husband and father mingling with the barking of a small, lovable dog.

Now as the winds of autumn sweep down into the valleys and rustle the leaves all about me, I swear I can hear a cacophony of sounds and the breeze whispering to the trees those very words I could never say: "I'm sorry!"

About the Author

John J. Koblas is the author and/or editor of six books on the lives of F. Scott Fitzgerald and Sinclair Lewis. His book, *F. Scott Fitzgerald in Minnesota: Toward the Summit,* published by North Star Press, was a 1996 Minnesota Book Award nominee. Other works include: *F. Scott Fitzgerald in Minnesota: His Homes and Haunts* (Minnesota Historical Society Press, 1978), *Sinclair Lewis: Home at Last* (Voyageur Press, 1981), *Selected Letters of Sinclair Lewis, Sinclair Lewis & Mantrap: The Saskatchewan Trip,* and *Sinclair Lewis: Final Voyage* (1985).

Five years ago, Mr. Koblas' work was featured on a television segment of *Good Morning America.* In 1985, he was a guest of Charles Kuralt on *CBS Sunday Morning* in New York for the Sinclair Lewis Centenary. That same year, Koblas was chosen by the Postmaster General in Washington to present the Sinclair Lewis Stamp at its First Day of Issue Ceremony. The following year, he received an award from the governor of Minnesota for his Fitzgerald work at the Minnesota Walk of Fame dedication.

In addition to biographical endeavors, Koblas has been a visiting instructor of writing at Brevard College in North Carolina, feature writer for the Daytona Beach (Florida) *News-*

Journal, and author of a syndicated column that was carried in 105 newspapers nationwide. He is the author of more than 500 short stories, articles, and verse published worldwide.

Recently, Mr. Koblas has taught courses on Fitzgerald and Lewis at the Elder Learning Center of the University of Minnesota and Elder Hostel sessions.

The Jesse James Northfield Raid: Confessions of the Ninth Man was published in 1999. This book is currently being filmed as a documentary by the Old West Society. Another book, *J.J. Dickison: Swamp Fox of the Confederacy,* will be published in 2000 by North Star Press. *H.V. Jones, an Adventure* will be published in 2001.

About the Artist

Born and raised in Daytona Beach, Florida, John Stevens became aware of his creative ability at the early age of five and developed a zest for the arts as he cultivated his talent. He won art contests in high school and continued to achieve recognition beyond that of his high school peers as Florida United States Senator Bob Graham's wife acquired one of his illustrations, a portrait of a child.

John Stevens graduated from college in his home town with a commercial art and advertising degree. His career in illustration blossomed as he easily won a prestigious award from L. Ron Hubbard Illustrators of the Future contest, an international contest for illustrators. His professional talent came to the attention of *Dell Magazine* where he is currently doing illustrations for their line of magazines while he works in a Florida advertising firm. This sought-after artist's work has been in North Star Press publications, *National Examiner*, and *Bride* Publication Incorporated, as well as in several books. John also takes time to teach portait drawing part time for Art Quest School of Art and Design, in Daytona Beach, Florida.

John is a member of the Association of Science Fiction and Fantasy Artists (ASFA) and Florida Motion Picture and Television Association (FMPTA). His work adorns the collections of Florida's United States Senator Bob Graham, Debbie Krick Fitness Classic (a top fitness competition), Kim Hartt of the Nevada Hot Dice RollerJam TV series, and Louise M. Kleba (A Systems Engineer at Boeing).

To contact the artist his address is: John Stevens, P.O. Box 9367, Daytona Beach, Florida 32120. E-mail: john@imagesofwonder.com